Current Chinese Economic Report Series

The Current Chinese Economic Reports series provides insights into the economic development of one of the largest and fastest growing economies in the world; though widely discussed internationally, many facets of its current development remain unknown to the English speaking world. All reports contain new data, which was previously unknown or unavailable outside of China. The series covers regional development, industry reports, as well as special topics like environmental or demographical issues.

More information about this series at http://www.springer.com/series/11028

Center for Macroeconomic Research at Xiamen
University

China's Macroeconomic Outlook

Quarterly Forecast and Analysis Report, February 2019

By the China's Quarterly Macroeconomic Model
(CQMM) Team

Springer

Center for Macroeconomic Research at
Xiamen University
Xiamen, Fujian, China

Grants: the major projects of China National Social Science Foundation (15ZDC011), the major research projects of philosophy and social sciences of China's Ministry of Education of China (16JZD016), the key research projects of the Key Research Institutions of Humanities and Social Sciences at Universities (17JJD790014, 18JJD790007, 18JJD790008), the project of China National Social Science Foundation (17BJY086), the project of China Natural Science Foundation (71503222, 71740022).

ISSN 2194-7937 ISSN 2194-7945 (electronic)
Current Chinese Economic Report Series
ISBN 978-981-13-9356-3 ISBN 978-981-13-9357-0 (eBook)
https://doi.org/10.1007/978-981-13-9357-0

This Springer imprint is published by the registered company Springer Nature Singapore Pte Ltd.
The registered company address is: 152 Beach Road, #21-01/04 Gateway East, Singapore 189721, Singapore

Preface

This report is a partial result of the China's Quarterly Macroeconomic Model (CQMM), a project developed and maintained by the Center for Macroeconomic Research (CMR) at Xiamen University. The CMR, one of the key research institutes of Humanities and Social Sciences sponsored by the Ministry of Education of China, has been focusing on China's economic forecast and macroeconomic policy analysis, and it has started to develop the CQMM for purpose of short-term forecasting, policy analysis, and simulation since 2005.

Based on the CQMM, the CMR and its partners hold press conferences to release forecasts for China's major macroeconomic variables. Since July, 2006, twenty-six quarterly reports on China's macroeconomic outlook have been presented and thirteen annual reports have been published.

This report, the twenty-sixth quarterly report, has been presented at the Forum on China's Macroeconomic Outlook and Press Conference of CQMM on February 26, 2019. This conference was jointly held at Beijing, China, by Center for Macroeconomic Research at Xiamen University and Economic Information Daily of Xinhua News Agency.

Xiamen, China

Center for Macroeconomic Research
at Xiamen University

Contents

Principal Investigator

Min Gong

Members of the Research Team

Zhiyuan Lin, Yu Liu, Yanwu Wang, Huakun Wu, Changlin Yu, Shengrong Lu, Guifu Chen, Jing Li, Wenpu Li, and Yanping Huang.

The Chinese edition of this report is due to Min Gong, Yanwu Wang, Huakun Wu, Changlin Yu, and Zhiyuan Lin. The English edition of this report is translated by Yu Liu and Yanping Huang. The raw data are processed by Huakun Wu.

Executive Summary

In 2018, China's economy achieved stable growth. The economic structure continued to improve. The employment remained stable. The key tasks of "three cuts, one reduction, one complement"[1] were firmly advanced, and the asset–liability ratio of enterprises, especially state-controlled enterprises, continued to decline.

In 2019, structural problems will bring changes in what is a generally stable economic performance, some of which causes concern. The external environment will be complex and severe, and the economy will face downward pressure.

First, a weakening global economic expansion in the next two years will put more downward pressure on export-oriented manufacturing investment growth and could reverse the recovery growth that private investment and manufacturing investment have started since 2017. Secondly, with the acceleration of the population aging, the growth rate of labor productivity has also slowed down, as well as the sharp rise of household debt ratio in the past two years, which will restrain the rapid growth of consumer expenditure. Finally, though the credit volumes have expanded tremendously over the past three years, the loans invested in the real economy have fell to 50%, and the share of loans invested in real estate and residential households has risen sharply. The investment of new RMB loans constitutes a serious distortion, which will not only reduce the efficiency of the use of credit resources, but also will inhibit the expansion of the investment of the real economy, will aggravate the bubble of the real estate market, and will further increase the systemic risk of the financial system.

At present, China and the USA's high-level trade negotiations are still under way. Despite positive signals from both sides, the possibility of failing to reach an agreement remains open. Therefore, the research team sets up two possible scenarios for China and US trade talks and forecasts China's macroeconomic trends accordingly.

---

[1] Supply-side structural reform: cutting overcapacity, de-stocking, de-leveraging, reducing costs, and improving underdeveloped areas.

Scenario One assumes that China and the USA would have successfully reached a trade agreement, thereby the two sides removing punitive tariffs previously imposed on each other from the second quarter of 2019.

Scenario Two pessimistically assumes that China and the USA would have failed to reach a trade agreement, thereby fulfilling the trade friction escalation measures originally scheduled from January 1, 2019.

The main performance of the China's macroeconomy over the next two years is forecast as follows.

(1) The GDP Growth
Forecast based on CQMM model shows that China's economic growth will continue to slow down in the next two years. Under scenario one, the real GDP is expected to grow by 6.4% in 2019, a decline of 0.2% points over 2018. Under scenario two, the real GDP growth will be reduced by an additional 0.16% points.

(2) The Investment Growth
Although the slowdown in global economic expansion in the next two years will dampen the growth of export-oriented manufacturing investment, the new round of infrastructure investment expansion initiated since the end of 2018 and the robust and positive monetary policy of 2019 will largely reverse the declining trend in investment growth, if China and the USA succeed in reaching a trade deal. Non-state investment will grow at a slow pace in the next two years, and the growth rate is likely to continue. Fixed asset investment (excluding farmers) is expected to grow 7.25%, up 1.23% points over the previous year. State-owned investment is expected to grow 7.21%, while non-state investment is expected to grow 7.42%.

(3) The Consumption Growth
The growth rate of resident income will continue to be stable with a slight decline in the next two years. With the rapid rise in household debt ratio in recent years, consumer spending is expected to be hard to grow rapidly. In 2019, per capita real disposable income of urban residents will rise 6.03%, an increase of only 0.43% points over 2018. Per capita cash income of rural residents will rise 8.16%, down 1.75% points. Retail sales of consumer goods are expected to grow 8.92% in nominal terms, down 0.13%.

(4) The Price Indexes
CPI is expected to rise 2.01%, down 0.14% points over the previous year, while PPI is expected to rise 1.40, down 2.13% points.

(5) The Import and Export Growth
Total export in current US dollar is expected to grow by 4.42% in 2019, down 5.42% points over the previous year. Total import is expected to grow by 10.72%, down 5.12% points. Net export growth will fall to −0.10% of GDP, down 0.80% points.

The forecast shows that weakening global economic expansion in the next two years, falling growth in domestic investment, and the difficulty of rapid growth in real income will place greater downward pressure on the Chinese economy. In the short term, maintaining an appropriate and stable rate of economic growth is of great practical significance for stabilizing employment, promoting the improvement of resident income, and tamping down the foundation of economic transformation. In the long run, for the purpose of pursuing high-quality development, it is necessary to promote the industrial transformation and upgrading through effective investment, to promote the consumption growth and consumption upgrading through the long-term sustained and rapid growth of labor productivity, and to promote the transformation of economic growth mode. Therefore, in 2019, the central government will continue to promote the "six-stable"[2] work plan proposed and to support private enterprise financing through financial support, such as tax cuts and fees reductions. These policies will undoubtedly stabilize and boost market confidence and promote rapid growth in private investment.

However, corporate profit growth, particularly in manufacturing, fell sharply in 2018. The concerns about trade friction between China and the USA will reverse the rising trend in private investment growth since 2017. Based on this, the research team proposed that in 2019, China should also lighten the burden of enterprises through reducing the social insurance contribution rate, in addition to continuing to implement a large-scale inclusive tax reduction policy. To achieve stable investment and stable employment, China should enhance the competitiveness of enterprises, as well as promote the effective investment growth of enterprises.

Let us turn to the burden of social insurance. First, reducing the contribution rate of social insurance will increase the profit of enterprises, which can promote the investment, drive the economic growth, and then improve the growth rate of financial revenue of governments. Second, reducing the contribution rate of social insurance will reduce the cost of employment, encourage the enterprise to expand employment, increase the income of residents, increase the consumption of residents, and improve the structure of total demand. Finally, the decrease of enterprise cost burden and the increase of profit will benefit the growth of R&D investment and then promote the technological progress and labor productivity.

In recent years, with the acceleration of the population aging, premium of the basic old-age insurance or pension insurance is growing quickly. Therefore, the social insurance burden borne by the enterprises and individuals is also increasing rapidly. In order to simulate the macroeconomic effects of reducing social insurance contribution rate, the research team conducts the following counterfactual analysis assumptions: The pension insurance contribution per participant is assumed to remain at 3750.9 yuan in 2015, 2016, and 2017, though the true premium were 3750.9, 4279.4, and 5727.5 yuan in the three years, respectively. Under this

[2] "Six-stable" work plan was proposed by the central government in the end of 2018: stable employment, stable foreign trade, stable investment, stable finance, stable foreign investment, and stable expectations.

assumption, the burden of businesses and individuals in 2016 and 2017 will be reduced by 469.125 billion yuan and 1227.47 billion yuan, respectively.

On this basis, the research team sets up two scenarios.

Scenario One is to refund or transfer the reduction of the social insurance contribution, 469.125 billion yuan in 2016 and 1227.47 billion yuan in 2017, to the enterprises as their profit.

Scenario Two is to transfer the reduction of the social insurance contribution to the residents as their labor remuneration.

It is found that, under either scenario, such a transfer is helpful to economic growth, resident consumption, and fiscal revenue. At the same time, because it can effectively reduce the cost burden of enterprises, it can also encourage enterprises to increase investment, and then promote employment and increase the resident income.

In addition, the transfer of the reduced social insurance contribution to the enterprise as its profit is more helpful to promote the investment growth of the enterprise and then produce a greater effect of fiscal revenue and short-term economic growth. To transfer of the reduced social insurance contribution to the residents as their labor remuneration will promote the growth of resident consumption, improve the overall demand structure, and achieve the rebalancing adjustment of the economic structure. Therefore, from the perspective of high-quality growth, the transfer of reduced social insurance contribution to the residents will undoubtedly produce better policy results.

Overall, export-oriented manufacturing investment growth will face greater downward pressure in the next two years, as global economic expansion slows down. The model forecasts that non-state-owned investment will continue to grow at a slow pace in the next two years, and that the growth is difficult to rebound quickly. Since the existing investment-driven growth pattern has not completely changed, if the growth rate of non-governmental investment could not rebound rapidly, then the cycle of "stable growth," "broad credit," " highly leverage of the local governments, of the state-owned and of the real estate companies," "household high debt ratios," "tight credit, financial consolidation," and "slower growth" would be hard to crack.

In beginning of 2019, the central government has issued a series of policies, such as tax cuts, to fully support the financing of private enterprises for a sustained, stable, and rapid growth of private investment. These policies certainly caught the crux of the problem and found a breakthrough to solve the above policy implementation difficulties.

We come up with the following policy recommendations.

First, fully supporting the financing of private enterprises will not only help achieving the short-term goal, but also help achieving the long-term goal.[3] Therefore, current policies, such as financial support, tax cut, and fees reduction, should focus on crowding out inefficient investment, encouraging enterprises to

[3] Short-term goal is stable investment, and long-term goal is enhancing the competitiveness of enterprises.

increase investment in R&D, enhancing competitiveness, and promoting industrial transformation and upgrading, in order to achieve sustained and rapid labor productivity growth.

Secondly, monetary policy should maintain reasonably sufficient liquidity while controlling the total amount and provide conditions for stable and efficient investment growth. While maintaining a reasonable increase of the credit, the social financing, and the broad money M2, emphasis should be placed on adjusting the structure of credit allocation to ensure that at least 60% of the loans go to non-financial enterprises or institutional groups, in order to truly support the financing of the real economy. At the same time, the financial service should be improved through mechanism innovation to support the real economy.

Thirdly, China should continue to implement a large-scale inclusive tax cut and fee reduction policy to reduce the macrotax burden of businesses. In 2017, the broad government revenue accounted for 34.4% of GDP. It was 3.2% points higher than that in the USA, 2.4% points higher than the average of emerging or developing economies, and 4.3% points lower than the average of developed economies. It shows that there is still room for the reduction of macrotax burden.

Fourthly, starting from 2019, the social insurance contribution will be collected by the tax authorities of the country. In order to promote the development of small- and medium-sized enterprises to achieve stable growth, China should reduce the social insurance contribution rate appropriately, lighten the burden of enterprises, and reduce the cost of enterprises.

Fifthly, China should be very vigilant against the negative impact of the rapid rise of household debt ratio on the consumer expenditure. With acceleration of the population aging, the social insurance system has not yet been perfected, and the income gap between urban and rural areas is still severe. As the growth rate of labor productivity slows down, it is difficult for the real income of residents to increase rapidly. Therefore, a rapid increase of household debt ratio will restrain the growth of resident consumption and hinder the transformation of economic growth mode.

Chapter 1
Review of China's Macroeconomy in 2018

In 2018, the real gross domestic product (GDP) of China grew 6.6%, an increase of 0.2% points over the previous year (Fig. 1.1). The economic growth continued to be stable with a slight decline. On the one hand, the key tasks of "three cuts, one reduction, one complement"[1] were firmly advanced, the asset-liability ratio of enterprises, especially state-owned holding enterprises, continued to decline, the employment remained stable, and the economic structure continued to be optimized. On the other hand, the weakening of the global economic expansion and the uncertainty of China and the United States trade friction, the sustained slowdown of domestic investment and the difficulty of increasing the growth of resident income placed a great downward pressure on economic growth.

Fig. 1.1 Growth rate of real GDP. *Source* CEIC

[1] Supply-side structural reform: Cutting overcapacity, de-stocking, de-leveraging, reducing costs and -improving underdeveloped areas.

China's Macroeconomic Outlook, Current Chinese Economic Report Series,
https://doi.org/10.1007/978-981-13-9357-0_1

1.1 The Economic Structure Optimized

The economic structure continued to be optimized, and the contribution rate of the tertiary industry to GDP growth had increased substantially.

In 2018, the economic structure of China continued to be optimized and adjusted to ensure a stable recovery of economic growth. The tertiary industry accounted for 52.2% of GDP, a slight increase of 0.3% points over the previous year. Owing to the steady growth of industrial production, the secondary industry accounted for 40.7% of GDP, an increase of 0.1% points over the previous year. The share of the primary industry continued to decline (Fig. 1.2).

The continuous increase in the share of tertiary industry to GDP had ensured the growth of new employment. At the same time, the contribution rate of the tertiary industry to GDP growth was also rising. On the other hand, the contribution rate of the secondary industry to GDP growth had continued to decline (Fig. 1.3). Since 2015, the contribution rate of the tertiary industry to GDP growth reached 55%, which had exceeded that of secondary industry. The contribution rate of the secondary industry to the growth of GDP continued to decline. The contribution rate of the tertiary industry to the growth of GDP was 59.7%, an increase of 6.7% points over 2015. The contribution rate of secondary production to GDP growth was 36.1%, down 6.4% points over 2015. Though the share of secondary industry to GDP was basically stable, its contribution rate to GDP growth had dropped substantially. This

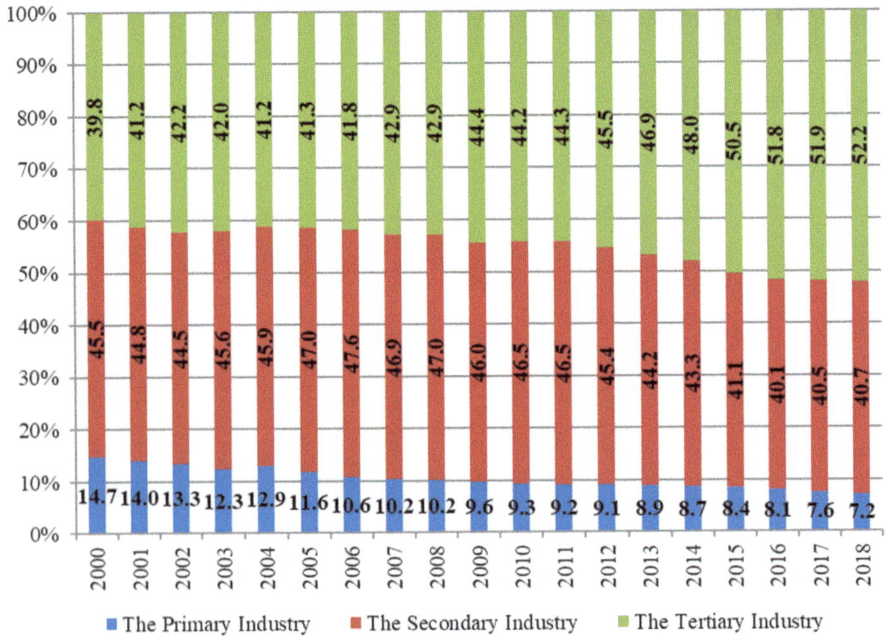

Fig. 1.2 The share of the three industries in GDP. *Source* CEIC

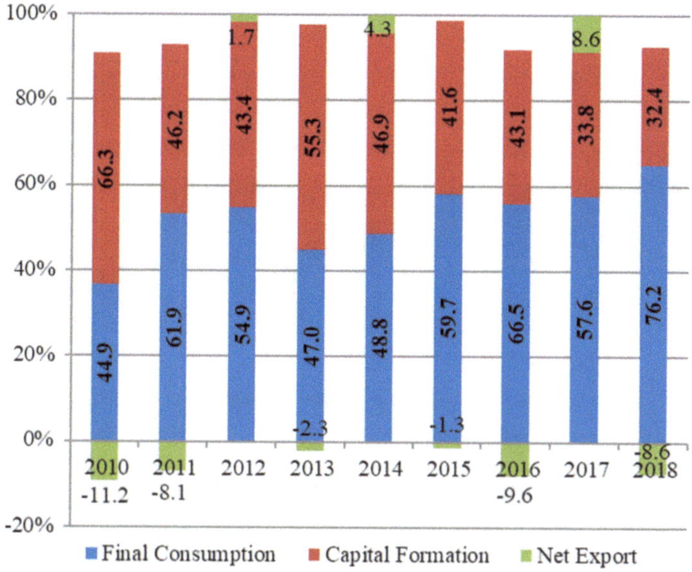

Fig. 1.3 The contribution to GDP growth. *Source* CEIC

fact, to a large extent, reflected the low efficiency of industrial production and the need for further advancement of industrial structure adjustment.

1.2 The Growth Rates of Investments Varied

The growth rate continued to slow down on fixed assets investment, dropped sharply on state-owned enterprises investment and recovered slowly on infrastructure and non-governmental investment.

In 2018, private investment and manufacturing investment continued to recover, while real estate investment grew at a steady pace. However, the investment growth rate of infrastructure and that of state-owned and state-controlled enterprises fell sharply. Fixed investment growth continued to decline. Fixed asset investment grew 5.9% in 2018, down 1.3% points over the previous year. The continued declining trend in investment growth since 2010 has not stopped.

In terms of ownership (Fig. 1.4), the investment of state-owned and state-controlled enterprises increased by 1.9%, a sharp drop of 8.2% points over the previous year. Private investment grew 8.7, 2.7% points higher than the previous year. State-owned and state-controlled enterprises accounted for 37.3% of the total investment, and private investment accounted for 62%, an increase of 0.5 and 1.6% respectively over the previous year. It is worth noting that private investment growth has gradually recovered since 2016, but the outbreak of trade frictions between China and the United States have begun to curb the growth of private investment led by

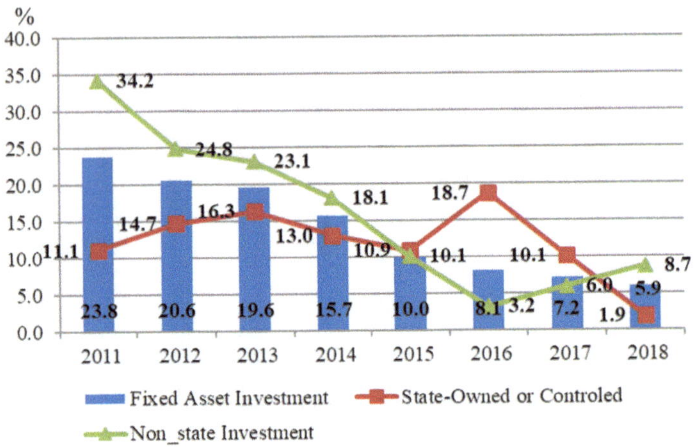

Fig. 1.4 The growth rate of fixed asset investment. *Source* CEIC

manufacturing exports. The sustainable and restorative growth of private investment will be an important factor in the steady growth of investment growth in the next two years.

In terms of the investment industries (Fig. 1.5), the financial regulatory policies adopted by governments at all levels to guard against financial risks and to reduce leverage have greatly inhibited the growth of infrastructure investment. Infrastructure investment increased 3.8% in 2018, down 15.2% points over the previous year. Infrastructure investment accounted for 22.9% of total investment, up 0.7% points over the previous year. Manufacturing investment grew 9.5%, up 4.7% points over the previous year. Manufacturing investment accounted for 33.4% of total investment, up 2.7% over the previous year. Despite the implementation of strict real estate regulation and control policies, real estate investment growth was still rapid, and its growth rate was 8.3%, an increase of 4.7% points over the previous year. Real estate

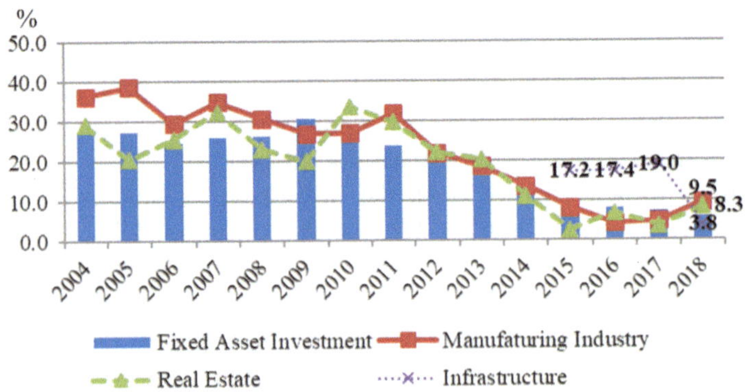

Fig. 1.5 Investment growth rates. *Source* CEIC

investment accounted for 23.8% of the total investment, 1.7% points higher than the previous year.

Overall, in the next two years investment growth downward pressure will be still very large. The weakening of the global economic expansion and the uncertainty of the China and the United States trade frictions will put a greater downward pressure on China's export-oriented manufacturing investment growth. After the growth of manufacturing investment and private investment hit their lowest growth rate in 2016, led by the expansion of the global economy, the growth rate of manufacturing investment, dominated by private capital, has begun to increase steadily. The growth rates of manufacturing investment have been higher than that of fixed asset investment in the whole society in either 2017 or 2018. However, the uncertainty over Sino-US trade frictions will likely reverse the restorative growth that private and manufacturing investment has started.

1.3 The Industrial Production Grew Steadily

Industrial production continued to grow steadily, profit growth rate of enterprises fell sharply.

Industrial production continued to grow steadily in 2018, but remained at its slowest pace since 2000 (Fig. 1.6). For the whole year, industrial value-added grew 6.2%, down 0.4% points over the previous year. Among them, the industrial value-added of state-owned and state-controlled enterprises increased 6.2%, down 0.3% points over the previous year. The industrial value-added of private enterprises increased 6.2%, an increase of 0.3% over the previous year. Industrial value-added of foreign businesses, Hong Kong, Macao and Taiwan investment enterprises grew 4.8%, down 2.1% points over the previous year. Since 2015, the growth rate of industrial value-added of state-owned and state-controlled enterprises, foreign investors and Hong Kong, Macao and Taiwan investment enterprises has changed from rapid rebound to steady growth, while the growth rate of industrial value-added of private enterprises has changed from continuous decline to steady growth.

While industrial production continued to grow steadily, the asset-liability ratio of state-owned and state-controlled enterprises declined (Fig. 1.7). The asset-liability ratio of industrial enterprises in 2018 was 56.5%, a slight increase of 0.6% points over the previous year. Among them, the asset-liability ratios of state-owned, state-controlled and large or medium-sized industrial enterprises were 52.6, 58.7, and 57.7%, respectively, down 0.7, 1.8 and 1.9% points over the previous year. In contrast, the asset-liability ratio of private industrial enterprises has continued to rise in the past two years, which was 56.4% in 2018, 3.8 and 5.7% points higher than in 2017 and in 2016.

Global economic expansion, which began in 2017, has slowed and the impact of weakening external market demand on manufacturing production and exports was gradually emerging. Since the second half of 2018, the manufacturing purchasing managers index (PMI) began to decline slowly, to 49.4% at the end of the year.

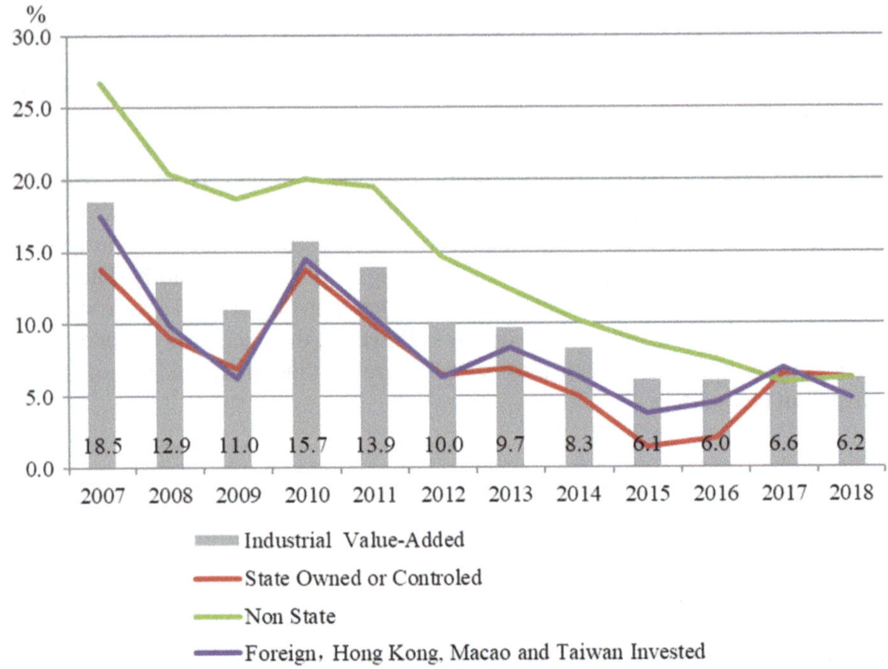

Fig. 1.6 The real growth rate of industrial value-added. *Source* CEIC

Among them, new manufacturing order PMI dropped to 49.7 and export order PMI fell sharply to 46.6 (Fig. 1.8). This indicated that the impact of the slowdown in external economic expansion and the escalation of trade frictions between China and the United States on China's manufacturing exports was gradually emerging, and this situation will continue in 2019.

Notably, profit growth of enterprise began to decline sharply (Fig. 1.9) in 2018. Profit of industrial large enterprises rose 10.3%, down 10.7% points over the previous year. Among them, profit of state-owned enterprises increased by −5.7%, a sharp decline of 45.6% points over the previous year, and profit of state-owned holding enterprises grew by 12.6%, down 32.5% points over the previous year. Profit of large and medium-sized state-controlled enterprises rose 11.2%, down 38.4% points over the previous year. Profit of private enterprises rose 11.9%, up only 0.2% points over the previous year.

Profit of manufacturing industry rose 8.7% in 2018, down 9.5% points over the previous year (Fig. 1.10). Among them, the profit of the general equipment manufacturing industry increased 7.3%, the profit of the specialized equipment manufacturing industry increased 15.8%, the profit of the automobile manufacturing industry increased −4.7%, the profit of the electrical machinery and equipment manufacturing industry increased 1.0%, and the profits of the computer, communication and other electronic equipment manufacturing industry rose by −3.1%, while those in the instrument manufacturing industry rose 6.9%. These growth rate fell by 6.2, 13.5,

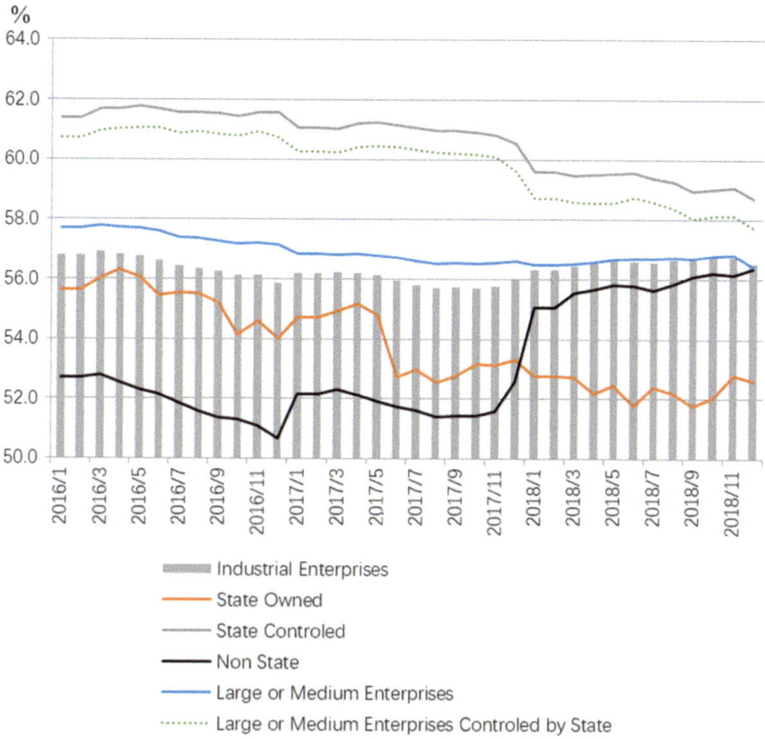

Fig. 1.7 The asset-liability ratio of industrial enterprises. *Source* CEIC

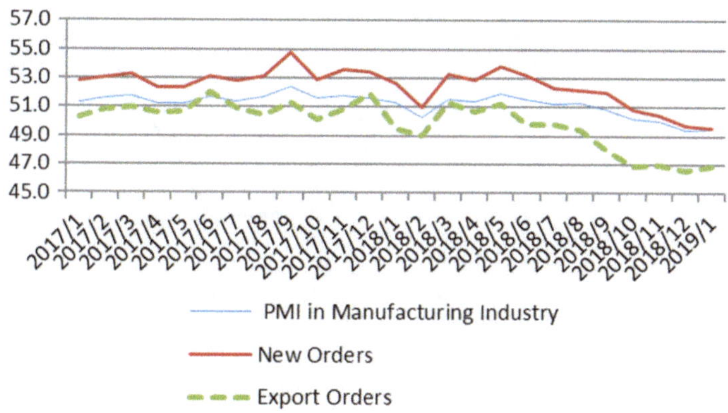

Fig. 1.8 Purchasing Manager Index in Manufacturing Industry. *Source* CEIC

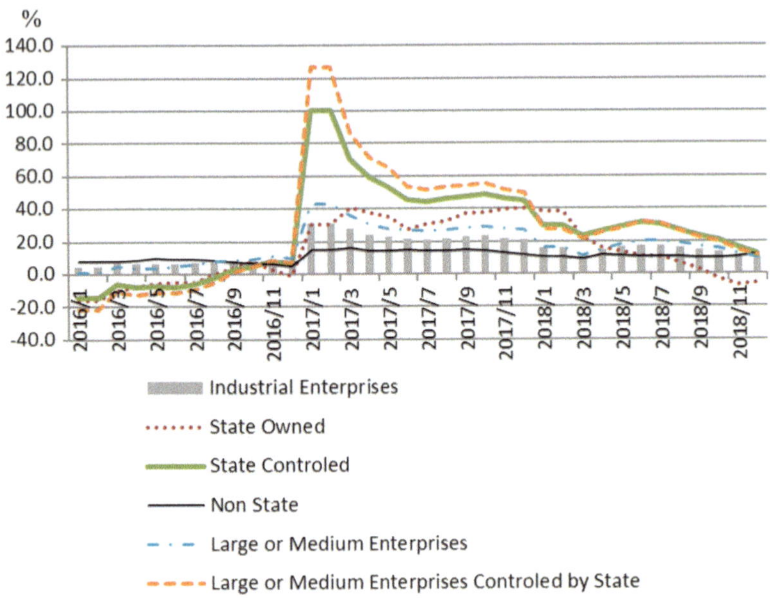

Fig. 1.9 Profit margin change of industrial enterprises. *Source* CEIC

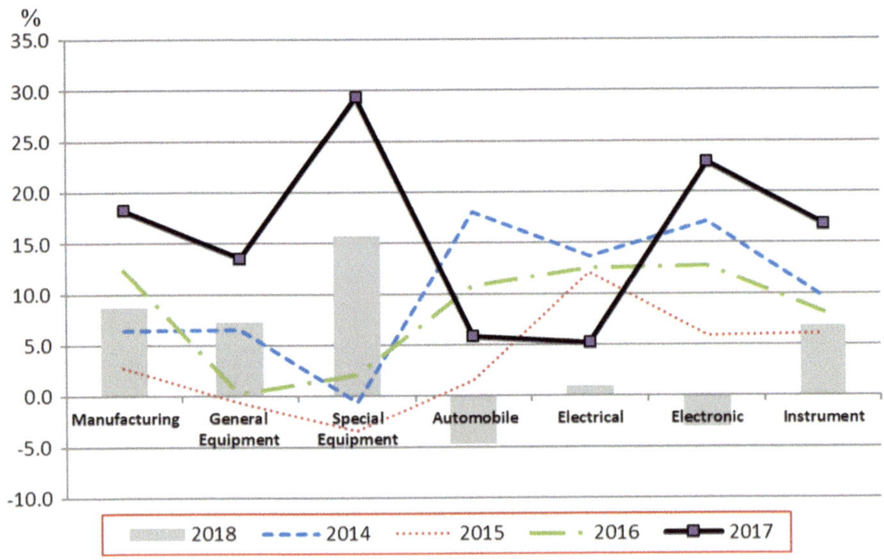

Fig. 1.10 Profit growth in major manufacturing industries.

10.5, 4.2, 26 and 9.9% points respectively over the previous year. In addition to the base effect, the decline in the growth rate of manufacturing profits in 2018, the sharp fall in export order PMI and the slowdown in consumption growth in the domestic market were among the main reasons. Profit growth in manufacturing, including manufacturing of cars, electrical machinery, communications devices, electronic devices and computers other, has been a five-year low.

Although industrial production continued to grow steadily in 2018, growth remained at its slowest pace since 2000. The weakening of the global economy has put downward pressure on export-oriented manufacturing production. The decline in manufacturing profit growth will dampen the rapid growth in manufacturing investment and fiscal revenue in the next two years.

1.4 The Growth of Import and Export Slowed Down

The growth rate of import and export slowed down, and the depreciation of RMB did not cause capital flight.

In 2018, China's import and export growth rate has slowed down. Exports rose 7.1%, down 3.7% points over the previous year, and imports rose 12.9%, down 5.8% over the previous year. The trade surplus reached 2.3303 trillion yuan, down nearly 521.62 billion yuan over the previous year (Fig. 1.11).[2]

The structure of trade continued to adjust, and the general trade as a share of total exports continues to rise in 2018. The general trade export in current US dollar

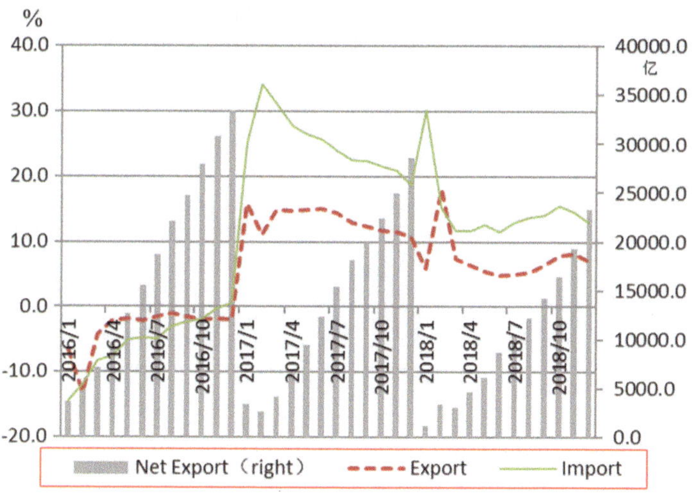

Fig. 1.11 Cumulative growth rate of import and export (RMB) and trade balance. *Source* CEIC

[2]In the first half of 2018, the price index of China's import and export trade both fell, and to a certain extent, it also lowered the growth rate of imports and exports.

accounted for 56.7% of the total export, up 1.9% points over the previous year. Processing export accounted for 32.0%, down 1.6% points. General trade imports accounted for 59.5, up 0.9% points. Processing import accounted for 22.0%, down 1.5% points over the previous year. The general trade surplus reached $140.58 billion, or 40. 0% of the total trade surplus, up 1.8% points over the previous year.

In terms of ownership the enterprises, the exports of private enterprises in US dollar accounted for 45.9% of the total exports in 2018, an increase of 1.5% points over the previous year. Exports of foreign-invested enterprises accounted for 41.7%, down 1.5% over the previous year, and state-owned enterprises accounted for 10.3%, roughly the same as the previous year.

In terms of import, the imports by private enterprises in US dollar accounted for 28.6% of total imports, up 1.5% points over the previous year; foreign-invested enterprises accounted for 43.6%, down 3.1% points; and state-owned enterprises accounted for 25.6%, up 1.9% points.

In the past two years, export of private enterprise has been playing an increasingly important role, for the share of export of private enterprises continued to exceed that of foreign-invested enterprises.

Since the central bank launched the reform of the intermediate pricing mechanism of the exchange rate in August 2015, the unilateral appreciation of the RMB against the US dollar has been effectively reversed, and the RMB exchange rate against the US dollar has begun to float bilaterally, with basic stability (Fig. 1.12). By the end of 2018, the dollar had a median price of 6.863 yuan against the RMB, and the yuan had depreciated 5.46% against the dollar in the year to the end of 2018, due to factors such as a rise in interest rates in the US dollar. With a sustained slowdown in the economy, the devaluation of RMB did not trigger large-scale capital flight, and the foreign exchange reserves reached 3.07 trillion dollar at the end of 2018, down 67.24 billion dollar over the previous year.

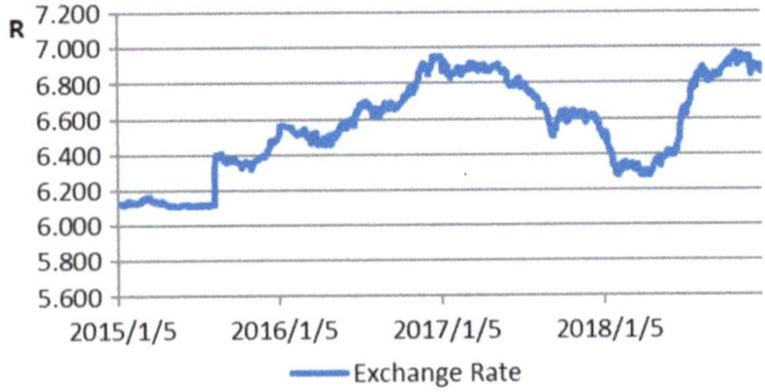

Fig. 1.12 The midpoint rate of the RMB against the US dollar. *Source* CEIC

1.5 The Growth of Consumption Slowed Down

CPI rose mildly, PPI fell back, real incomes grew steadily and the growth of consumption slowed down.

Consumer price continued to rise mildly in 2018, with CPI reaching 2.1%, an increase of 0.5% points over the previous year. The core CPI, which excludes food and energy, reached 1.9%, down 0.3% points over the previous year. In 2018, the fluctuating international oil prices largely curbed the rise in the Producer Price Index (PPI). PPI rose to 3.5%, down 2.8% points over the previous year (Fig. 1.13).

In 2018, resident income continued to grow steadily. The per capita real disposable income of the whole country increased 6.5%, down 0.8% points over the previous year. The per capita real disposable income of urban and rural residents increased 5.6 and percent respectively, down 0.9 and 0.7% points respectively (Fig. 1.14).

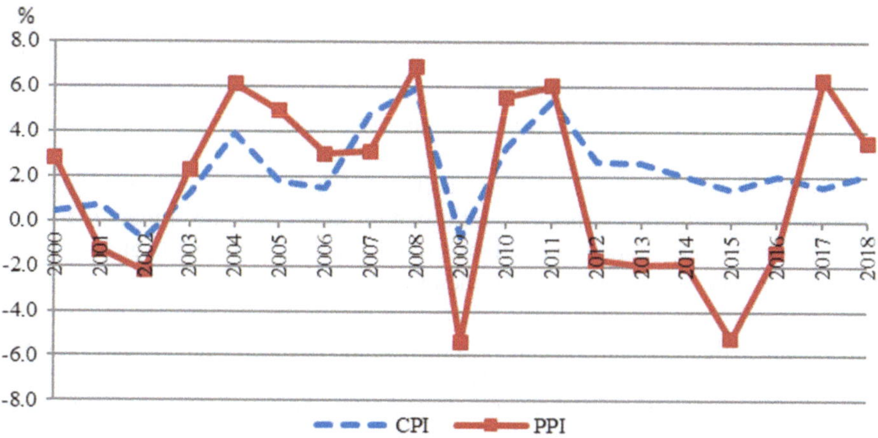

Fig. 1.13 Main price index change. *Source* CEIC

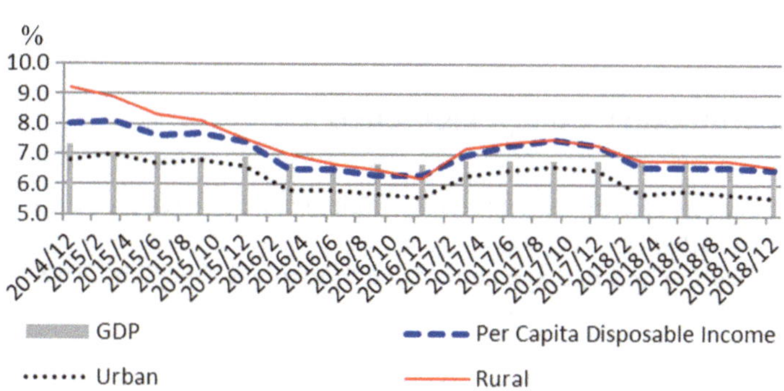

Fig. 1.14 GDP and the growth rate of per capita disposable income (price adjusted). *Source* CEIC

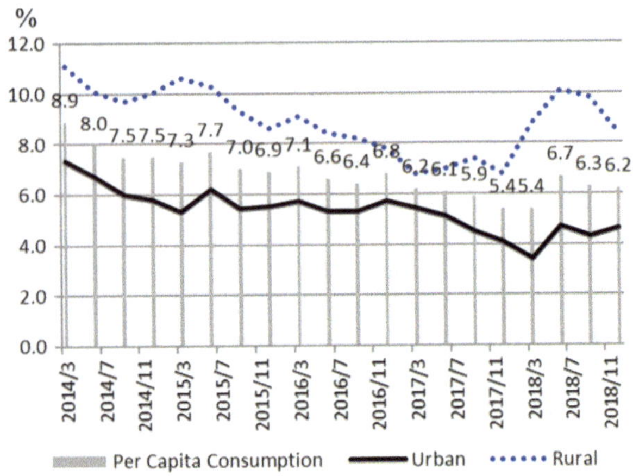

Fig. 1.15 Growth rate of per capita consumer expenditure (price adjusted). *Source* CEIC

Consumption growth slowed as real income growth slowed down. Retail sales of consumer goods rose 9% in nominal terms in 2018, down 1.2% points over the previous year. The real total retail sales of social consumer goods rose 6.9%, down 1.7% points. The per capita real consumption expenditure rose 6.2%, an increase of 0.8% points. Real consumer spending per capita in urban and rural areas rose 4.6 and 8.4% respectively, up 0.5 and 1.6% points (Fig. 1.15). Even so, per capita consumer spending growth in 2018, especially for urban residents, was lower than in 2015.

The slow decline in labor productivity growth in recent years has begun to restrain the rapid growth of real income, and then the rapid growth of consumption. In the long term, with the acceleration of population aging, the growth rate of consumer expenditure will be more difficult to increase rapidly. Fundamentally, at present, the rapid growth of labor productivity of the industries, especially manufacturing industries, should be the foundation to ensure the rapid increase of labor productivity and the real income growth rate of residents.[3] Therefore, how to expand the effective investment of manufacturing industry, promote industrial upgrading, and speed up the growth of labor productivity is a key issue to be solved.

1.6 The Monetary Policy Tightened

The monetary policy tightened, the composition of allocation of credit resource needs to be adjusted urgently

The rectification and management of the "Financial chaos" in 2018 has led to a sharp decline in the ability for banks to derive credit through non-bank channels. M0 increased 3.6% for the whole year, up 0.2% points over the previous year; M1 grew 1.5%, down 10.3% points; and M2 grew 8.1%, the same pace as the previous year.

[3]Research team, Macroeconomic Research Center, Xiamen University. China Macroeconomic Forecast and Analysis-Spring 2018 report.

New social financing totaled 19.3 trillion yuan in 2018, down 3.1 trillion yuan over the previous year. Of these, new RMB loans totaled 15.7 trillion yuan, an increase of 1.8 trillion yuan over the previous year. New RMB loans accounted for 81.4% of total social financing, up 19.6% over the previous year and it was the highest since 2010 (Fig. 1.16).

Due to the extreme expansion of credit volumes over the past three years, the composition of new RMB loans has been distorted: the loans invested into the real economy has fallen sharply and its share was under 50%, but the share of loans invested into real estate and residential households has increased significantly. Though the size of new RMB loans in 2018 has nearly doubled to the level of 2012, for loan as a share, the real economy accounted for 51.4%, down 17.6% points from 2012, and the share of loans to real estate rose to 39.9%, up 23.4% points from 2012 (Fig. 1.17).[4]

The serious distortion of the investment of RMB loans in the past three years not only has directly led to inefficiency of the use of credit resources, but also has inhibited the expansion of investment demand in the real economy, and aggravated the expansion of the bubble in the real estate market and raised the systemic risk of the financial system. Further, the household debt ratio has been significantly increased, thus curbing the rapid growth in consumer spending.[5] It is urgent to adjust the structure of credit resources.

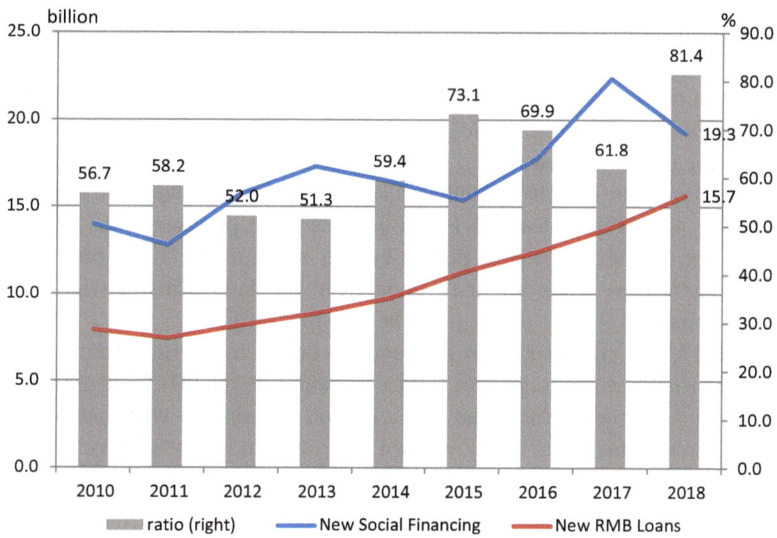

Fig. 1.16 The total amount of new social financing and new total amount of RMB loans. *Source* CEIC

[4]The share of loans to households rose sharply to 45.5%, up 14.8% points from 2012.

[5]Research team, Center for Macroeconomic Research, Xiamen University: China's Macroeconomic Forecast and Analysis-Autumn 2018.

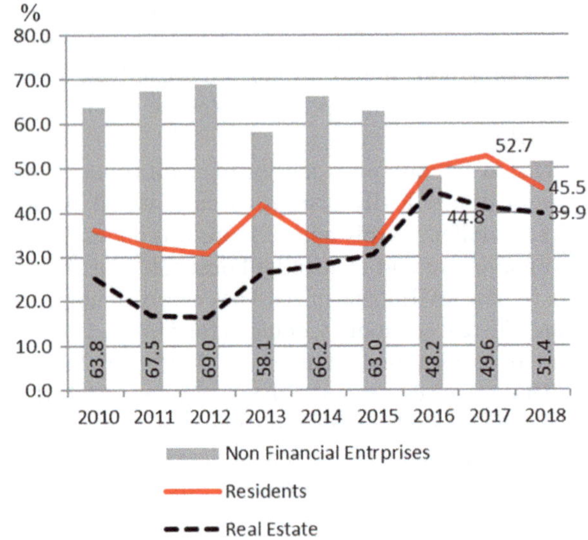

Fig. 1.17 The composition of New RMB loan Investment. *Source* CEIC

1.7 The Growth of Fiscal Revenue Declined

The growth rate of fiscal revenue declined, and the income from land transfer greatly increased.

In 2018 in nominal terms,General public budget revenue grew 6.2%, down 1.9% points over the previous year, while general public budget expenditure grew 8.8%, up 0.6% over the previous year (Fig. 1.18). Affected by the decline of profit growth of state-owned and state-controlled enterprises, tax revenue growth also slowed down. Tax revenue rose 8.3%, down 2.4% points over the previous year. Tax revenue accounted for 85.3% of general public budget revenue, up 1.2% points over the previous year. Local government revenue from the land transfer was 6.5 trillion yuan, an increase of 25.0% points over the previous year.

Since 2013, the growth rate of tax revenue began to decline from double-digit to single-digit. Tax revenue growth fell to 4.8 and 4.4% in 2015 and 2016, a nearly 30-year low. At present, under the financial and tax system with industrial tax as the main source of taxation, the slowdown of growth in industrial production and in the corporate profits have greatly curbed the growth of tax revenues. Therefore local governments have to expand land transfer income, such as restricting land supply or obtain loan resources through land mortgage. This directly increases the debt burden of local governments and, in turn, increases the risks of the financial system.

Overall, while China's economy achieved stable growth in 2018, the economic structure continued to optimize, the employment remained stable, and the key tasks of "three cuts, one reduction, one complement"[6] were firmly advanced. The asset-

[6]Supply-side structural reform: Cutting overcapacity, de-stocking, de-leveraging, reducing costs and -improving underdeveloped areas.

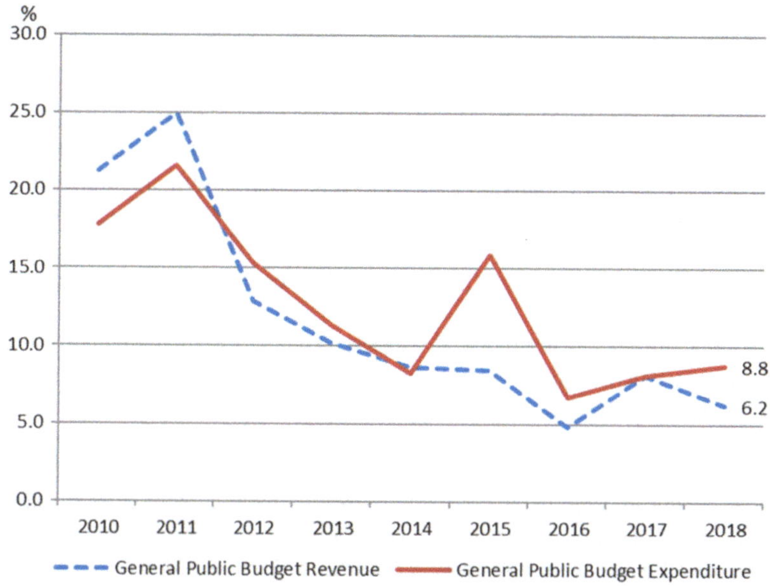

Fig. 1.18 Growth in general public budget revenue and expenditure. *Source* CEIC

liability ratio of enterprises, especially state-owned holding enterprises, continues to decline. At the same time, the downward pressure on economic growth remains strong.

First, the growth rate of investment in fixed assets continued to decline. In 2018, private investment and investment in the manufacturing sector continued to recover; the growth rate of real estate investment was basically stable, and the growth rate of investment in infrastructure investment and investment in state-owned and state-controlled enterprises fell sharply. As a result, the fixed investment growth rate continued to decline. In the next two years, the weakening of the global economic expansion and the uncertainty of the China and the United States trade frictions will put a greater downward pressure on China's export-oriented investment growth in the manufacturing sector. It is also likely to reverse the recovery growth that has begun in private and manufacturing investment since 2017.

Second, growth in corporate profits fell sharply in 2018. Industrial production grew steadily, the asset-liability ratio of state-owned and state-controlled enterprises has fallen, and the corporate profit growth has slowed sharply. The weakening of the global economic expansion in the next two years will further put downward pressure on export-oriented manufacturing production. The decline in manufacturing profit growth and the lack of a rapid rebound in private sector profit growth will dampen the rapid growth in manufacturing investment and revenue growth in the next two years.

Third, the growth rate of per-capita consumption expenditure of the residents was gradually slowing down. With the acceleration of population aging, the growth rate of the labor productivity in China has been decreasing, and the increase in the household debt ratio will slowdown in the past two years.

Fourth, the investment of the new RMB loan should be adjusted urgently. Over the past three years, while the total amount of credit has been tremendously expanded, the share of loans invested into the real economy has fallen sharply, which was close to 50%; and the share of loans invested into real-estate and residential households has been significantly increased. This not only reduced the efficiency of the credit resources, but also restrained the expansion of the real economy investment, aggravated the bubble of the real estate market, and further increased the systemic risk of the financial system.

After 2015, the decline in private investment growth directly dampened the growth in manufacturing investment, which in turn led to a decline in industrial value-added growth. From the perspective of steady investment, in order to offset the decline in the growth rate of non-governmental investment, governments have to expand their investment in infrastructure, and have to strengthen the investment of state-owned enterprises in the monopolistic fields, including real estate. This directly raised the debt ratio of governments and state-owned enterprises. From the point of view of fiscal revenue, the decline in the growth of industrial value added directly restrained the growth of revenue of governments, increased the dependence of governments on land transfer income, and thus fostered the bubble of the real estate market. From the point of view of the allocation of credit resources, the decline of profit margin in manufacturing and the rising debt ratio of enterprises led to the difficulty for the credit resources to enter the real economy. The expanded credit either was idle within the financial system, or was sucked into the real estate sector or lent to the residential sector, leading to a sharp rise in household debt. The increase in household debt ratio has begun to restrain the growth of consumer spending when the real income growth rate was difficult to increase rapidly. Since the existing investment-driven growth pattern has not completely changed, if the growth rate of non-governmental investment could not rebound rapidly, then the cycle of "stable growth", "broad credit", "highly leverage of the local governments, of the state-owned and of the real estate companies", "household high debt ratios", "tight credit, financial consolidation" and "slower growth" would be hard to crack.

At the end of 2018, governments restarted the expansion of infrastructure investment for steady growth. In 2019, a series of financial support, tax cuts, comprehensive support for private enterprise financing policies have been introduced. These policy measures certainly caught the crux of the problem, and found a breakthrough to solve the above policy implementation difficulties. Considering that the weakening of the global economic expansion in the next two years will continue to restrain the growth of China's manufacturing profits, the research team proposes that while continuing to implement a large-scale inclusive tax reduction policy at the present time, China should also reduce social insurance contribution rate appropriately, lighten the burden of enterprises, reduce the cost of enterprises, promote the effective investment growth of enterprises, enhance the competitiveness of enterprises, achieve stable investment and stable employment. Based on this, this research team attempted to study the macro-economic impact of reducing the social insurance contribution rate of enterprises.

Chapter 2
China's Macroeconomic Forecast for 2019–2020

2.1 Assumptions of Model Exogenous Variables

2.1.1 Economic Growth Rates

Since the end of 2018, the downward pressure on global economic growth has been increasing, and the weakening trend of economic expansion is becoming more and more obvious. In the United States, as the effects of stimulus policies recede, the process of reducing balance sheet and raising interest rates has begun to slow down. Growth in the Eurozone has fallen to a four-year low, owing to a slowdown in Germany and Italy, coupled with an increase in the likelihood of a "hard Brexit". The World Economic Outlook, published by the International Monetary Fund (IMF) in January 2019, predicts that the US economy will probably grow by 2.5 and 1.8% in 2019 and 2020. After lowering its forecast for Eurozone growth, the IMF expects the Eurozone to grow 1.6 and 1.7%, respectively, in the next two years.

Given the possibility of a positive outcome in the current China and the United States trade talks, the research team sets the U.S. economic growth rate to be 2.68 and 1.89% in the next two years, slightly higher than the IMF forecast. Based on the forecast of the United States Congressional Budget Office, the research team sets the growth rate for each quarter (Fig. 2.1). On the other hand, although trade frictions between the United States and Europe over cars and parts are likely to escalate, trade relations between the Eurozone and other regions, such as China, are relatively stable. Therefore, the research team sets economic growth rate of the Eurozone to be 1.73 and 1.70% for the next two years, slightly higher than the IMF forecast. With reference to the European Central Bank's forecast, the research team sets the growth rate for each quarter (Fig. 2.1).

China's Macroeconomic Outlook, Current Chinese Economic Report Series,
https://doi.org/10.1007/978-981-13-9357-0_2

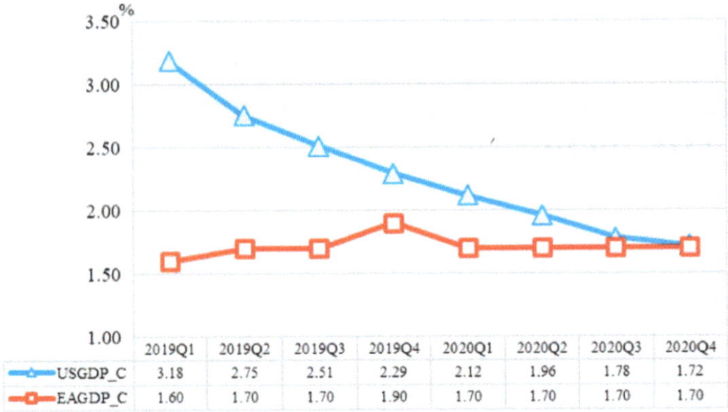

	2019Q1	2019Q2	2019Q3	2019Q4	2020Q1	2020Q2	2020Q3	2020Q4
USGDP_C	3.18	2.75	2.51	2.29	2.12	1.96	1.78	1.72
EAGDP_C	1.60	1.70	1.70	1.90	1.70	1.70	1.70	1.70

Note: EU_GDP_C represents the growth rate of real GDP in the Eurozone, and US_GDP_C represents the growth rate of real GDP in the United States.

Fig. 2.1 Assumptions of the economic growth rate of the United States and the Eurozone. *Source* Assumption of Research team

2.1.2 The Exchange Rates

Since 2018, the dollar index has continued to rise, leading to a sustained strengthening of the dollar against the Euro and the RMB. In 2019, though the Fed's rate-raising process is likely to slow, higher uncertainty about Eurozone economic growth could keep the Euro stable with slight decline. By the end of 2020, the Euro is expected to convert to 1.13 dollar (Fig. 2.2). On the other hand, since the RMB intermediate

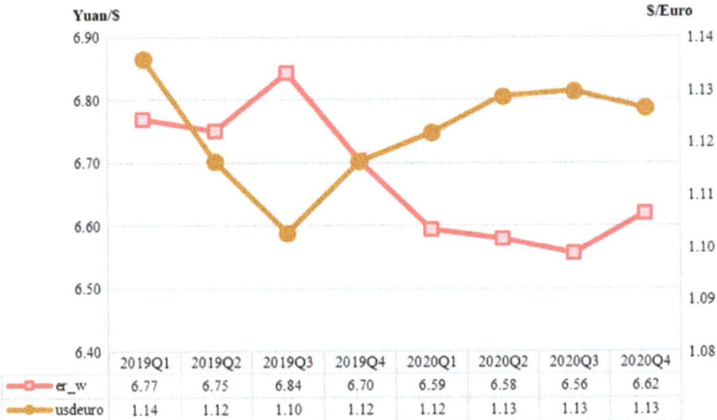

	2019Q1	2019Q2	2019Q3	2019Q4	2020Q1	2020Q2	2020Q3	2020Q4
er_w	6.77	6.75	6.84	6.70	6.59	6.58	6.56	6.62
usdeuro	1.14	1.12	1.10	1.12	1.12	1.13	1.13	1.13

Note: usdeuro represents the exchange rate of the Euro against the US dollar, er_w represents the exchange rate of the US dollar against RMB.

Fig. 2.2 Assumed changes in the exchange rate of the Euro against the US dollar and the exchange rate of the US dollar against RMB. *Source* Assumption of Research team

pricing mechanism was launched in August 2015, the RMB exchange rate has remained bilateral floating and basically stable against the US dollar. The trend is expected to continue at 6.70 yuan per dollar by the end of 2019 and may change to 6.62 yuan by the end of 2020 (Fig. 2.2).[1]

2.1.3 Growth Rate of Broad Money Supply (M2)

In 2018, to rectify the “financial chaos”, to guard against risks, to reduce leverage, strict financial regulatory policies were implemented, resulting in a sharp decline in the ability for banks to derive credit through non-bank channels. The growth rate of M2 was only 8.1% in 2018. The money supply is expected to grow in the next two years, taking into account the complex and volatile external economic environment and growing downward pressure on the economy. The research team assumes M2 growth could rise to 9.0% in 2019 and 9.3% in 2020 (Fig. 2.3).

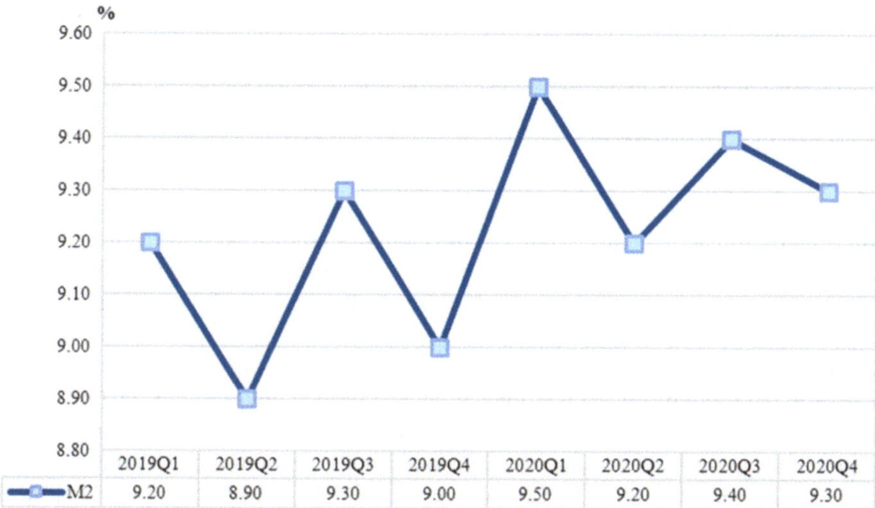

Fig. 2.3 M2 growth rate trend assumption. *Source* Assumption of Research team

[1]By the end of January 2019, the dollar had a median price of 6.703 yuan against the RMB, up 2.1% from the beginning of the month.

2.2 Two Scenarios on the China and the United States Trade Talk

At present, China and the United States high-level trade talk is still under way. Despite positive signals from both sides, the possibility of failing to reach an agreement remains open. Based on this, the research team sets up two scenarios for China and the United States trade talk and then forecasts China's macroeconomic trends. One is the optimistic scenario (**scenario one**), in which the two sides lift punitive tariffs imposed on each other when a successful trade agreement is reached. Specifically, in the first quarter of 2019, the United States still imposed a 25% tariff on $50 billion of Chinese exports to the United States, and a 10% tariff on an additional 200 billion dollar of Chinese exports to the United States. China has accordingly imposed a 25% tariff on 50 billion dollar imports from the United States and a 10% tariff on an additional 60 billion dollar imports from the United States, but since the second quarter, both sides will no longer impose punitive tariffs on each other.[2]

The second is a pessimistic scenario (**scenario two**), in which China and the United States fail to reach a trade agreement, and the trade friction escalation measures will be delivered. Though the first quarter of 2019 was the same as scenario one, since the second quarter, the United States would impose a 25% tariff on 250 billion dollar of Chinese exports to the United States, while China would correspondingly impose a 25% tariff on total 110 billion dollar on imported goods from the United States, and it would last until 2020.

The impact of the escalation of China and the United States trade friction on China's macro-economy is as follows: First of all, the increase in punitive tariffs will directly impact China's exports to the United States (as well as China's imports from the United States). After tariffs have changed the relative prices of Chinese exports (and imports), the indirect effect of trade friction will begin, and then it will further affect China's exports and imports with other countries and regions. Secondly, although with the transformation and upgrading of the domestic economic structure, the trend of internalization and localization is obvious, since China is still in the middle and lower reaches of the global industrial chain. Although the share of processing trade has declined significantly, it still accounts for about 30% of the total export. The reduction in China's exports to the United States will lead to a reduction in imports of raw materials and primary products, thereby maintaining a certain degree of stability in net exports. Finally, and most importantly, in the long run, escalating trade frictions will dampen investment expansion in China's export-

[2]The punitive tariff increase was set in the second quarter of 2019, a slight deviation from the current Trump-declared deadline for negotiations March 1, 2019. The reasons are as follows: first, due to the model and data constraints, can only be delineated into the quarterly field, so close from the second quarter. Given the inherent time lag of the economy, the error should not be too large. Second, the final dust set for trade negotiations could exceed the March 1 deadline. In fact, Trump himself has said he can consider a moderate relaxation of this limit. Nor can observers rule out the possibility of a phased agreement between the two sides before March 1 to secure more time for the details to be finalised according to what is known to the outside world.

oriented non-state manufacturing sector, which in turn will have a negative impact on domestic investment, employment and consumption.

Next, the research team will estimate the growth trend of China's macro-economy in 2019–2020 based on the CQMM model.

2.3 Forecast of Major Macroeconomic Indicators in 2019 and 2020

2.3.1 Forecast of GDP Growth Rate Under the Two Scenarios

Under the assumptions of these exogenous variables, forecasts based on CQMM show that if China and the United States succeed in reaching a trade agreement (scenario one), then China's GDP is expected to grow by 6.40 and 6.22% in 2019 and 2020, down 0.20 and 0.18% points over previous year, respectively. If China and the United States fail to reach a trade agreement (scenario two), then GDP growth could fall sharply to 6.24 and 6.27% in 2019 and 2020, down 0.36 and up 0.03% points lower, respectively.[3] This shows that the economic growth rate of China will continue to be stable with slight decline. The current downward pressure on China's economic growth is still due to a slowdown in domestic investment and consumption. The escalation of trade frictions between China and the United States in 2019 could further reduce GDP growth by an additional 0.16% points.

In term of the quarterly year-on-year growth rate, under scenario one, GDP growth presented a "first low and then high" situation in 2019. GDP growth is expected to slow to 6.24% in the first quarter compared to the same quarter of previous year, as punitive tariffs are still in place. Subsequently, the conclusion of a trade agreement will drive a gradual recovery in GDP growth. The third and fourth quarters are expected to be close to 6.5%. In 2020, the remaining economic structure problems and the weakening of global expansion will restrain the growth of GDP. The growth rate will be 6.39% in the first quarter, and about 6.1–6.2% for the rest of the quarter. Under scenario two, GDP growth in each quarter would fall further compared with scenario one (Fig. 2.4).

[3]In 2020, the GDP growth rate of scenario 2 was slightly higher than that of scenario 1 by 0.05% points. The size of GDP under scenario 2 in 2020 is actually lower than scenario 1.

	2019Q1	2019Q2	2019Q3	2019Q4	2020Q1	2020Q2	2020Q3	2020Q4
Scenario 1	6.24	6.40	6.49	6.46	6.39	6.15	6.13	6.20
Scenario 2	6.24	6.11	6.24	6.37	6.28	6.34	6.27	6.20

Fig. 2.4 Quarterly GDP Growth Forecast (Quarterly year-on-year Growth Rate) of the two scenarios. *Source* Calculated by the research team

2.3.2 *Forecast of Import and Export Growth Rate Under the Two Scenarios*

Under scenario one,[4] import and export growth would also drop significantly in the next two years. The total export and total import in US dollar will increase by 4.42 and 10.72% respectively in 2019. The two growth rates will be 4.00 and 14.34% in 2020, (Table 2.1).[5] Under scenario two,[6] import and export growth would also drop significantly in the next two years. The total export and total import in US dollar will increase by 2.23 and 8.98% respectively in 2019. The two growth rates will be 3.32 and 13.26% in 2020 (Table 2.1).

Under scenario one, China's export to the United States would grow by 5.28% in 2019, down 5.65% points over the previous year, and the growth rate would further slowdown to 4.68% in 2020. China's exports to the EU, ASEAN and other trading partners grew by 3.94, 7.09 and 3.63% respectively, down 6.05, 6.88 and 4.83% points over the previous year. In 2020, these growth rate would be 3.33, 6.39 and 3.33%, respectively.

Under scenario one, China's imports from the United States, would grow by 17.40% in 2019, up 17.0% points over the previous year, and it could fall to 11.96% in 2020. In 2019, the trade transfer effect could cause China's imports from the EU, ASEAN and other trading partners to rise 5.99, 6.62 and 11.82%, down 5.58, 7.97

[4]A successful trade agreement is reached between China and the United States

[5]In the second half of 2018, China's export enterprises exported ahead of the implementation of punitive tariffs, which to some extent led to the suppression of the growth space of exports in 2019.

[6]Failure to reach a trade agreement between China and the United States

Table 2.1 Forecast of China's import and export growth rate in 2019 and 2020: %

Year	Region	Export				Import			
		Current dollar		Current RMB		Current dollar		Current RMB	
		Scenario1	Scenario 2	Scenario1	Scenario 2	Scenario1	Scenario 2	Scenario1	Scenario 2
2019	Total	4.42	2.23	6.92	4.68	10.72	8.98	13.38	11.60
	US	5.28	−7.88	7.77	−5.71	17.40	2.85	20.66	5.70
	EU	3.94	5.87	9.63	9.60	5.99	5.82	9.22	7.38
	ASEAN	7.09	7.06	6.38	8.36	6.62	4.81	8.46	8.28
	Other	3.63	3.66	6.16	6.19	11.82	11.18	14.49	13.84
2020	Total	4.00	3.32	1.24	0.58	14.34	13.26	11.32	10.27
	US	4.68	0.22	1.91	−2.44	11.96	7.63	9.01	4.79
	EU	3.33	3.97	3.57	3.57	6.37	6.43	9.54	5.26
	ASEAN	6.39	6.38	0.59	1.22	12.51	8.12	3.56	3.62
	other	3.33	3.34	0.60	0.60	16.41	16.00	13.33	12.94

Source Calculated by the research team

and 7.24% points respectively over the previous year. In 2020, the corresponding growth rate was 6.37, 12.51 and 16.41% respectively.

However, under scenario two, the increase of tariff and overdraft of demand would lead to a decline in China's export to the United States to −7.88% in 2019, a 13.16% point lower than scenario one, and it is expected to rebound to 0.22% in 2020. China's exports to the EU, ASEAN and other trading partners are expected to grow 5.87, 7.06 and 3.66% in 2019, up 1.93, 0.03 and 0.03% points from scenario one, and will continue to decline slightly in 2020. China's imports from the United States are expected to grow at 2.85 and 7.63% in 2019 and 2020, down 14.55 and 4.33% points from scenario one, respectively, due to the punitive tariffs. China's import growth from other regions outside the United States will also face varying degrees of decline, with growth in imports from ASEAN expected to suffer a bigger impact (Table 2.1).

Finally, under scenario one, China's net exports are expected to fall to −0.10%, down 0.80% points over the previous year in 2019, and it could be further down to −1.90% in 2020. under scenario two, net exports would account for −0.18 and −1.83% of GDP for the next two years.

In either case, China's foreign exchange reserves are expected to remain above 3 trillion dollar this year.

2.3.3 *Forecast of Investment Growth Rate Under the Two Scenarios*

In 2018, the policies to guard against financial risks, tighten regulation, and de-leverage significantly curbed investment growth in infrastructure and state-owned enterprises. While the growth in private investment continued to recover, the growth total investment fell sharply throughout the year.

Under scenario one, investment in fixed assets (excluding farmers) would increase by 7.25% in 2019, 1.35% points higher than in 2018, and it would increase by 6.58% in 2020. Under scenario two, fixed asset investment would grow by 6.57 and 6.40% in 2019 and 2020, respectively. Therefore, the new round of infrastructure investment expansion starting at the end of 2018, the robust and aggressive monetary policy in 2019 and efforts to avoid escalating trade frictions would help boost investment growth (Table 2.2).

In terms of quarterly year-on-year growth, under scenario one, In 2019, fixed asset investment growth could be 5.32% in the first quarter and it would reach 9.63% in the third quarter. It would be between 6.40 and 6.92% in 2020. Under scenario two, a deeper decline in the growth rate of non-state-owned investment led to a decline in investment growth in all quarters compared with scenario one (Fig. 2.5).

In terms of ownership, the sharp decline in the growth rate of profits of state-owned enterprises in 2018 largely led to a sharp decline in the growth rate of investment in state-owned enterprises. Investment growth in state-owned enterprises is expected to

Table 2.2 Forecast of investment growth rate (current value) in 2019 and 2020: %

	TI_C_SA		FAI_SA		FAI_SOE_SA		FAI_PRI_SA	
Quarter	Scenario one	Scenario two	Scenario one	Scenario two	Scenario one	Scenario two	Scenario one	Scenario two
2019	2.28	2.17	7.25	6.57	7.11	7.21	7.42	6.26
Q1	1.67	1.67	5.32	5.32	2.92	2.92	7.33	7.33
Q2	3.05	2.97	7.67	6.71	6.68	6.71	8.27	6.71
Q3	2.48	2.34	9.63	8.72	10.43	10.63	8.01	6.45
Q4	1.93	1.73	6.44	5.58	8.56	8.75	6.12	4.63
2020 年	1.83	1.62	6.58	6.40	7.44	7.42	6.07	5.79
Q1	1.87	1.62	6.40	5.52	6.60	6.72	6.27	4.80
Q2	1.82	1.61	6.40	6.49	7.67	7.77	5.64	5.72
Q3	1.82	1.63	6.92	6.94	7.77	7.59	6.41	6.55
Q4	1.79	1.62	6.62	6.64	7.71	7.57	5.95	6.07

Note TI_C_SA is the fixed-value fixed of asset investment (expenditure method), FAI_SA indicates the current value of fixed-asset investment, FAI_SOE_SA means the state-owned and state-owned holding fixed asset investment. FAI_PRI_SA is the part of fixed asset investment that deducts state-owned and state-owned holdings
Source Calculated by the research team

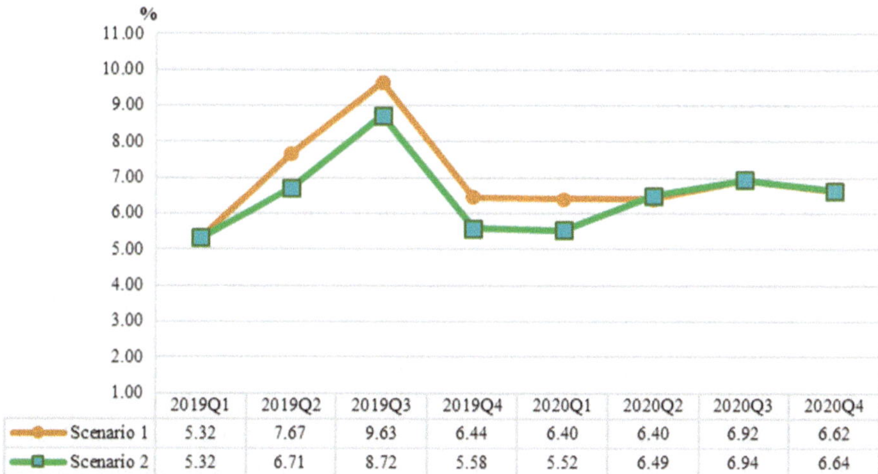

Fig. 2.5 Fixed asset investment growth forecast (quarterly year-on-year growth rate). *Source* Calculated by the research team

rebound to a certain extent in the next two years. Under scenario one, state-owned investment is expected to grow 7.11% in 2019, up 5.21% points over 2018, and it is expected to be 7.44% in 2020. Under scenario two, the goal of stable growth could prompt faster growth in state-owned investment, which is expected to grow 7.21 and 7.42% in 2019 and 2020, respectively (Table 2.2).

On the other hand, the slowdown in global economic expansion in the next two years will dampen China's import and export growth and, in turn, export-oriented growth in private investment in manufacturing. Under scenario one, non-state investment is expected to grow 7.42% in 2019, down 1.28% points over 2018, and it could fall to 6.07% in 2020. Under scenario two, non-state investment is expected to grow 6.26% in 2019 and further decline to 5.79% in 2020 (Table 2.2).

Overall, although the slowdown in global economic expansion in the next two years will dampen the growth of export-oriented manufacturing investment, the new round of infrastructure investment expansion initiated since the end of 2018 has seen a robust and positive monetary policy in 2019. Under scenario one, it would largely reverse the declining trend in investment growth, but non-state investment would grow at a slow pace in the next two years, and it would be unlikely to rebound quickly.

2.3.4 *Forecast of Growth Rate for Other Macroeconomic Indicators*

For the sake of brevity, the forecast only reported the results of scenario one, because the results would be no significant difference under the two scenarios.

(a) The main price index forecast

CPI would reach 2.01% in 2019, down 0.12% points over 2018, and would fall to 1.86% in 2020. CPI is expected to rise first and then decline in each quarter in the next two years, returning to a steady trend (Fig. 2.6). PPI would rise to 1.40% in 2019 and fall to 1.34% in 2020. The growth rate would gradually recover in 2020 after hitting a low in the third quarter of 2019 (Fig. 2.6). The GDP deflator (PGDP) would rise to 2.12 and fall to 2.00% in 2019 and 2020, and it would reach a peak in the second quarter of 2019 before recovering to stabilize (Fig. 2.6). Overall, the inflation level of China's economy will be within the controllable range in the next two years.

(b) Forecast of resident income and consumption

The real per capita disposable income for urban residents would rise 6.03% in 2019, up 0.43% points over 2018, and it would rise 5.85% in 2020. On the other hand, per capita cash income for rural residents is expected to grow 8.16% in 2019, down 1.75% points over 2018, and it would rebound slightly to 8.44% in 2020 (Fig. 2.7). Therefore, the real income of residents would continue to grow steadily in the next

	2019Q1	2019Q2	2019Q3	2019Q4	2020Q1	2020Q2	2020Q3
CPI_SA	2.06	2.39	1.84	1.75	1.80	1.76	1.87
P_P_SA	1.64	1.84	0.93	1.21	1.28	1.33	1.34
PGDP_SA	2.10	2.25	2.27	1.88	1.94	1.92	2.00

Note: CPI_SA, P_P_SA and PGDP_SA represent seasonally adjusted consumer price index, producer price index and GDP deflator index respectively.

Fig. 2.6 Price Index Forecast (Quarterly year-on-year growth rate). *Source* Calculated by the research team

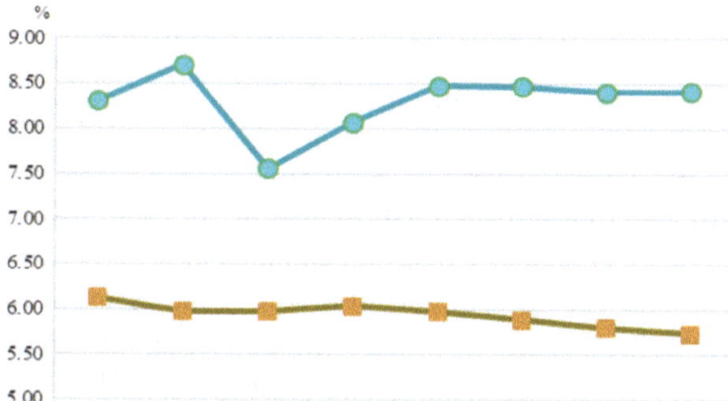

	2019Q1	2019Q2	2019Q3	2019Q4	2020Q1	2020Q2	2020Q3	2020Q4
YD_U_C_PC	6.13	5.98	5.98	6.04	5.98	5.89	5.80	5.74
YC_R_C_PC	8.31	8.71	7.56	8.07	8.48	8.47	8.41	8.42

Note: YD_U_C_PC indicates per capita real disposable income for urban residents and YC_R_C_PC for per capita cash income of rural residents.

Fig. 2.7 Forecast of income of urban and rural residents. *Source* Assumption of the research team

two years, but the growth rate of rural residents would be difficult to increase rapidly and the gap between urban and rural income would be difficult to narrow rapidly.

China's household debt ratio has risen rapidly in recent years, which has restrained the rapid growth of consumer spending. The model forecasts a nominal growth rate of 8.92% for retail sales of consumer goods in 2019, down 0.13% points over 2018, and the same growth rate in 2020 as in 2019. Consumer consumption in comparable price is expected to grow 5.42% in 2019, down 3.81% points over 2018, and is expected to rise to 6.94% in 2020 (Fig. 2.8).

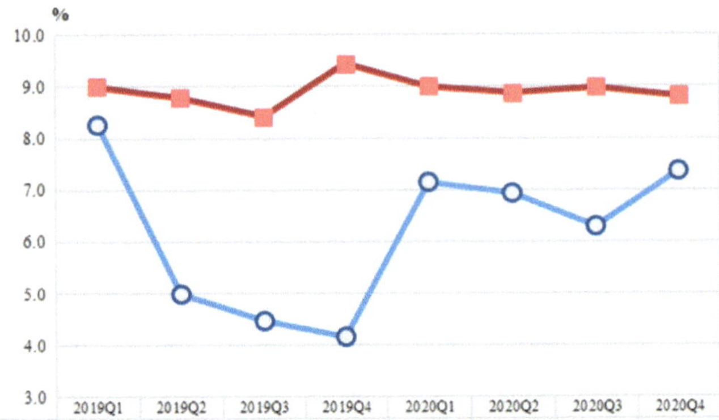

	2019Q1	2019Q2	2019Q3	2019Q4	2020Q1	2020Q2	2020Q3	2020Q4
RETAIL_SA	9.01	8.79	8.42	9.44	9.01	8.87	8.98	8.81
CON_D_C_SA	8.26	4.99	4.47	4.15	7.15	6.94	6.30	7.36

Note: RETAIL_SA represents the growth rate of total retail sales (current price) of social consumer goods; CON_D_C_SA indicates the growth rate of total consumer consumption (constant price).

Fig. 2.8 Consumption growth Forecast (Quarterly year-on-year growth rate). *Source* Calculated by the research team

Overall, the forecast based on CQMM model shows that China's economic growth would continue to slowdown in the next two years. The current downward pressure on economic growth continues to come from a slowdown in domestic investment and consumption. A further escalation in trade frictions between China and the United States in 2019 could push down GDP growth by an additional 0.16% points. The slowdown of global economic expansion would significantly restrain the growth of China's import and export. The start of a new round of infrastructure investment expansion since the end of 2018, the robust and aggressive monetary policies in 2019, and a successful trade deal between China and the United States could boost investment growth to a large extent. However, the slow growth of non-state investment in the next two years is likely to continue. The slow growth of the real income growth in China in the next two years and the rapid rise in the household debt ratio in recent years will make it difficult for consumer spending to grow rapidly.

Under scenario one, the model forecast results are summarized as follows:

1. Real GDP growth is forecast to be 6.4% in 2019, 0.2% points lower than in 2018; CPI 2.01, 0.14% points lower than in 2018; PPI 1.40, 2.13% points lower than in 2018.
2. Fixed asset investment (excluding farmers) is expected to grow 7.25% in 2019, up 1.23% points over the previous year; the state-owned investment by 7.21%; non-state-owned investment by 7.42%; the per capita real disposable income of urban residents by 6.03%, up 0.43% points; the per capita cash income of rural residents by 8.16%, down 1.75% points; the retail sales of consumer goods by 8.92% in nominal terms, down 0.13% points; the total export in US dollar by 4.42%, down 5.42% points; the total import in US dollar by 10.72%, down 5.12% points. The net exports are expected to fall to −0.10% of GDP, down 0.80% points over 2018.

Chapter 3
Two Scenarios to Analyze the Effects of Reducing Social Insurance Rate

The weakening of the global economic expansion, the decline in the growth rate of domestic investment and the difficulty of rapid growth in real income have placed greater downward pressure on the China's economy. In the short term, maintaining an appropriate and stable rate of economic growth is of great practical significance, in order to stabilize employment, to promote the improvement of resident income and to tamp down the foundation of economic transformation. In the long term, to pursue and promote high-quality development, it is necessary to promote the industrial transformation and upgrading through effective investment, and promote the consumption growth and consumption upgrading through the long-term sustained and rapid growth of labor productivity, so as to promote the transformation of economic growth mode. Based on this, in 2019, the central government will continue to promote the "six-stable"[1] plan, and tax cuts and fee reduction will provide support for private enterprise financing. These polices will stabilize and boost market confidence and promote rapid growth of private investment.

During the period from 2016 to 2018, through replacing business tax with VAT, reducing the VAT tax rate, increasing the tax exemption, increasing the tax cut, simplifying administrative procedure, reducing administrative fees and a series of preferential tax policies for small and micro-enterprises, China has achieved a tax cut of 0.6196 trillion yuan, 1 trillion yuan and 1.3 trillion yuan respectively in the past three years. Domestic tax cut and fee reduction, coupled with a synchronized recovery in the global economy, private investment growth began to recover after it reached the lowest in 2016.

However, corporate profit growth, particularly in manufacturing sector, fell sharply in 2018, and the uncertainty of trade friction between China and the United States reversed the recovery of private investment growth since 2017. For this reason, the research team proposes that in 2019, in addition to large-scale inclusive tax cut, China should lighten the burden of enterprises and reduce the cost of enterprises through appropriate reduction of social insurance contribution rate, in order to pro-

[1] six-stable: stable employment, stable finance, stable foreign trade, stable foreign investment, stable expectations.

China's Macroeconomic Outlook, Current Chinese Economic Report Series,
https://doi.org/10.1007/978-981-13-9357-0_3

mote the effective investment growth of enterprises, to improve the competitiveness of enterprises, and to achieve stable investment and stable employment.

For a long time, a large part of the corporate cost burden comes from the social insurance borne by the enterprises. In provincial capitals throughout the country, the social insurance contribution accounted for 38.82% of the employee's income in 2018. Such a high rate of social insurance has significantly increased the cost of employment and squeezed the profit of the enterprises.[2] Moreover, the increase in social insurance contributions rate may also offset the effect of tax cuts. Therefore, the broad-based tax burden costs borne by enterprises may not change. In order to give full play to the function of countercyclical adjustment of social insurance policy, the social insurance rate of enterprises should be properly adjusted to lighten the burden of enterprises, but not to affect the overall welfare of the insured.

First of all, reducing the social insurance contribution rate is beneficial to the increase of enterprise profit, which can promote the investment growth of enterprises, drive the economic growth, and then improve the growth rate of financial revenue. Secondly, reducing the cost of employment is also beneficial to the expansion of employment, to the increase of resident income and consumption, and to the improvement of the structure of total demand. Finally, the decrease of enterprise cost burden and the increase of profit growth will benefit the growth of R&D investment, and then promote the technological progress and labor productivity.

In view of this, in order to analyze the macroeconomic effect of reducing the social insurance contribution rate, the research team will use the CQMM model to simulate and analyze the economic effects that may be caused by reducing social insurance contribution rate.

3.1 The Total Amount and Structural Change of Social Insurance

The existing social insurance system was established in the 1990s. The social insurance includes basic pension insurance, basic medical insurance, unemployment insurance, employment injury insurance, maternity insurance, housing provident fund and

[2]Excessive nominal social security rates will also crack down on the enthusiasm of enterprises to participate in social security, forcing enterprises to evade, underreport, and understate social security contributions, seriously affecting the smooth operation of the social security system. Hinder the further expansion of social security coverage, increase the difficulty of social security collection, increase law enforcement costs. With the introduction of the reform plan of the national tax and local tax collection system, the social insurance contribution will be collected by the tax department from 2019. Compared with the social security department, tax departments have more means of collection and management, which cause many enterprises to worry about the rising burden of social security. In order to ease this concern, the State Council has made it clear that all localities should maintain the existing collection policy until the reform of the social security collection agency is in place, and it is strictly prohibited to centralize and clear fees owed by enterprises on their own. At the same time, we should study properly to reduce the social security rate to ensure that there is no increase in the burden on the enterprise as a whole.

it accounts for 38.82% of the total income of employees. The overall burden of enterprises is among the highest in the world.

First of all, in recent years, social insurance fund revenue has grown rapidly. According to statistics from the Ministry of Human Resources and Social Insurance, the income of China's social insurance fund was about 6715.42 billion yuan in 2017, 25.4 times as much as in 2000, with an average annual growth rate of 21.0%. The accumulated balance was about 7731.16 billion yuan. The gap between the annual revenue and accumulated balance of social insurance fund has continued to expand since 2007 (Fig. 3.1).

Secondly, the pension insurance and the medical insurance are the two main components of the social insurance fund. From 2000 to 2017, the pension insurance revenue and the medical insurance revenue as a share of social insurance fund revenue gradually increased from 92.6 to 96.1%. The pension insurance expenditure and the medical insurance expenditure as a share of social insurance fund expenditure gradually increased from 93.9 to 96.0%. Among these, the pension insurance revenue as a share of social insurance fund revenue gradually decreased from 86.1 to 69.4%. The pension insurance expenditure as a share of social insurance fund expenditure decreased from 88.7% to 70.7%. The medical insurance revenue as a share of social insurance fund revenue gradually increased from 6.4 to 26.7%. The medical insurance expenditure as a share of social insurance fund expenditure increased from 5.2 to 25.2% (Fig. 3.2).

Third, the differences of social insurance funds among provinces are significant. Taking pension insurance as an example, in 2017, the top six provinces[3] accounted

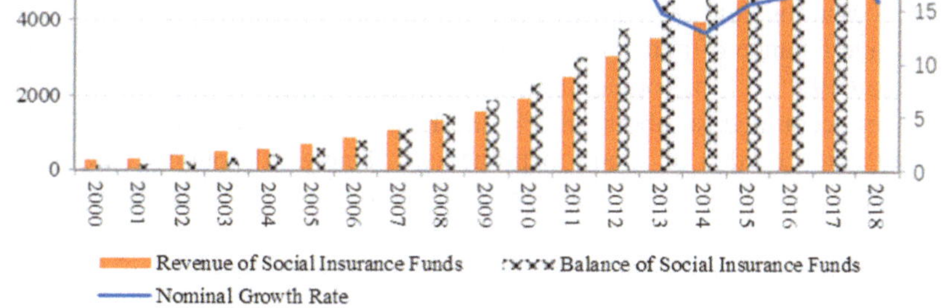

Note: 2018 social insurance fund revenue is based on the income of the basic pension fund and its share.

Fig. 3.1 Changes in annual income and accumulated balance of social insurance fund. *Source* CEIC

[3]Guangdong, Sichuan, Zhejiang, Jiangsu, Shanghai and Shandong.

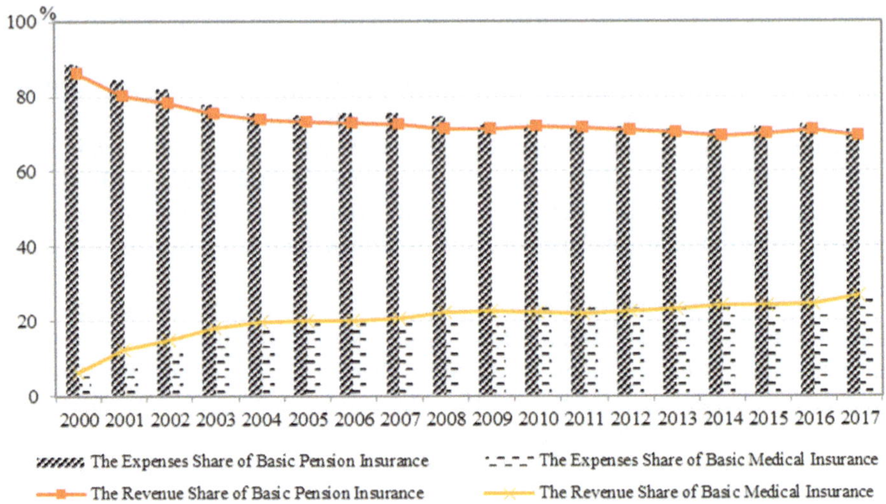

Fig. 3.2 The revenue-share and expenditure-share of basic pension or medical insurance. *Source* CEIC

for about 41.0% of the total pension insurance revenue of the whole country, while the last six provinces[4] accounted for 4.5%. The top six provinces accounted for 38.5% of total pension insurance expenditure of the whole country, while the latter six provinces accounted for just 4.5% (Fig. 3.3). The difference between revenue and expenditure of pension insurance in most provinces is basically small. Among them, the revenue exceeded the expenditure in 12 provinces. In Guangdong, Sichuan and Beijing, their revenues were 2.71, 1.58 and 1.33% points higher than their expenditures, respectively. In Liaoning, Heilongjiang, Shandong and Hubei provinces, the revenues were 1.47, 1.11, 0.70 and 0.69% points lower than expenditures, respectively.

Further, in terms of the cumulative balance of the pension insurance funds, the differences among the provinces were even more pronounced (Fig. 3.4). In 2017, the cumulative balance of pension insurance funds in Guangdong alone accounted for more than 19.2% of the total cumulative balance of the whole country. The top six provinces accounted for about 58.2%, and Heilongjiang accounted for −0.8%.

Finally, the burden of social insurance was heavy. Although China has implemented five cuts in social insurance contribution rate since 2015, overall, social insurance contribution rate for businesses and individuals are still high. In 2018, the social insurance contribution rate in all provinces were between 32.9 and 41.7%. (Table 3.1), with an average of about 38.82%.

The social insurance contribution rate borne by enterprises are different among regions. Shanghai is the highest, reaching 31.2%, while Guangdong is the lowest, about 22.7%. The social insurance contribution rate borne by individuals are not different very much among regions.

[4]Guizhou, Gansu, Hainan, Ningxia, Qinghai and Tibet.

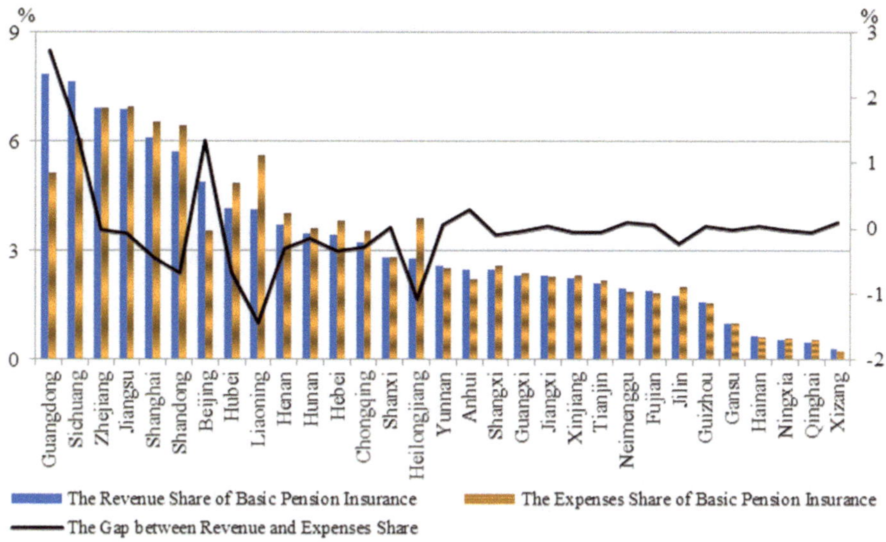

Fig. 3.3 The revenue-share and expenditure-share of the pension insurance by provinces in 2017. *Source* CEIC

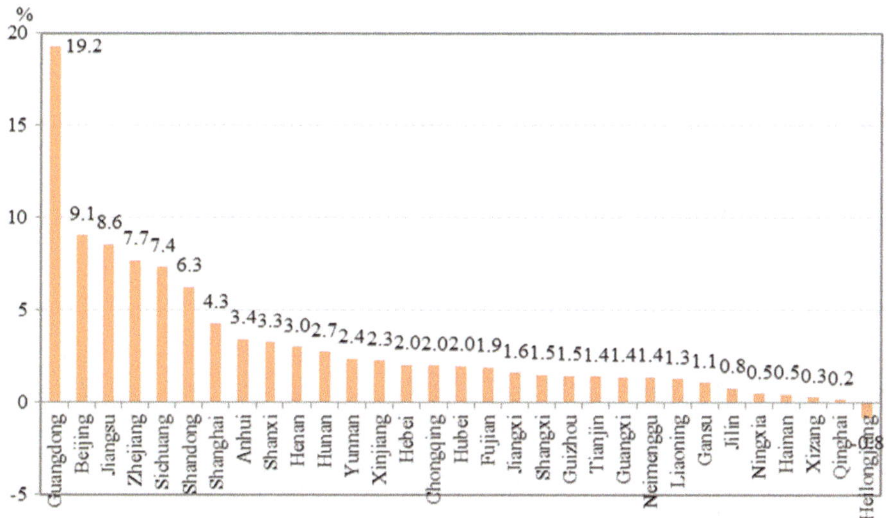

Fig. 3.4 The share of cumulative balance of basic pension funds of each provinces in 2017. *Source* CEIC

Table 3.1 Social insurance contribution rate in 2018: %

Province	Total social insurance rate			Pension insurance rate		Medical insurance rate	
	Total	Enterprises	Individual	Enterprises	Individual	Enterprises	Individual
Beijing	41.0	30.8	10.2	19.0	8.0	10.0	2.0
Tianjin	38.7	28.2	10.5	17.0	8.0	10.0	2.0
Hebei	40.2	29.9	10.3	20.0	8.0	8.0	2.0
Shanxi	37.7	27.4	10.3	19.0	8.0	7.0	2.0
Inner Mongolia	37.9	27.4	10.5	20.0	8.0	6.0	2.0
Liaoning	39.8	29.3	10.5	20.0	8.0	8.6	2.0
Jilin	38.9	28.6	10.3	20.0	8.0	7.0	2.0
Heilongjiang	39.3	28.8	10.5	20.0	8.0	7.5	2.0
Shanghai	41.7	31.2	10.5	20.0	8.0	9.5	2.0
Jiangsu	40.0	29.5	10.5	19.0	8.0	9.0	2.0
Zhejiang	36.9	26.4	10.5	14.0	8.0	10.5	2.0
Anhui	38.2	27.7	10.5	19.0	8.0	8.0	2.0
Fujian	37.7	27.2	10.5	18.0	8.0	8.0	2.0
Jiangxi	36.7	26.2	10.5	19.0	8.0	6.0	2.0
Shandong	39.2	28.9	10.3	18.0	8.0	9.0	2.0
Henan	39.2	28.9	10.3	19.0	8.0	8.0	2.0
Hubei	38.9	28.6	10.3	19.0	8.0	8.0	2.0
Hunan	38.9	28.6	10.3	19.0	8.0	8.0	2.0
Guangdong	32.9	22.7	10.2	14.0	8.0	7.0	2.0
Guangxi	39.0	28.5	10.5	19.0	8.0	8.0	2.0
Hainan	38.7	28.2	10.5	19.0	8.0	8.0	2.0
Chongqing	40.7	30.2	10.5	19.0	8.0	9.5	2.0
Sichuang	38.5	28.1	10.4	19.0	8.0	7.5	2.0
Guizhou	38.7	28.4	10.3	19.0	8.0	7.5	2.0
Yunan	40.1	29.8	10.3	19.0	8.0	9.9	2.0
Tibat	39.1	28.6	10.5	19.0	8.0	8.0	2.0
Shaanxi	39.5	29.2	10.3	20.0	8.0	8.0	2.0
Gangsu	39.2	28.9	10.3	19.0	8.0	8.0	2.0
Qinghai	37.6	27.1	10.5	20.0	8.0	6.0	2.0
Ningxia	39.2	28.7	10.5	19.0	8.0	8.0	2.0
Xingjiang	39.5	28.5	11.0	19.0	8.0	8.0	2.5
Average	38.82	28.40	10.42	18.81	8.00	8.11	2.02

Note According to the data from the website of the People's Social Affairs Department of each province, the level of the whole province is represented by the social insurance contribution rate of the provincial capital cities; the pension rate is calculated only for urban workers, but not for flexible employment personnel; the industrial injury insurance rate is calculated at the lowest 0.2%

The pension insurance rate and the health insurance rate borne by enterprises and individuals were about 26.81 and 10.13%, respective. They add up to 36.94%.

According to Liu Yanbin (2009), there are 13 countries in which all social insurance contribution rate (including pension insurance, medical insurance, industrial injury insurance, unemployment insurance and family allowance) were less than 10%, 43 countries between 10 and 20%; 33 countries between 20 and 30%; 26 countries between 30 and 40%; and only 12 countries higher than 40%. Similarly, according to Guambo (2016), China's social insurance contribution rate ranks 13th among the 173 countries listed, close to the 40% of the European high-welfare countries such as France, Germany and Italy. China's social insurance contribution rate is higher than the United States (16.05%), Japan (25.24%) and South Korea (15.13%), about 3.04 times as much as that of the Philippines, 3.84 times of Thailand and 4.76 times of Mexico. The nominal rate of "social insurance and house fund" has reached about 60%, if housing provident fund were included (about 10–24%).[5]

Wei Shengmin and Xiang Jing (2018) further summarized the comparison of social insurance contributions of enterprises among some countries (Table 3.2). It can be seen that although five previous fee reductions have been made, in China, social insurance contribution rate borne by enterprises companies are still as high as around 28.35–30.05%, not only higher than those in the United States, Japan and some developing countries, but also higher than European welfare countries such as Germany and Sweden.

On the one hand, an excessive social insurance contribution rate will increase of the cost of employment, squeeze the profit of the enterprises, weaken the investment ability of the enterprises, especially the high-tech enterprises, which is not conducive to the technological innovation and the improvement of the competitiveness of the enterprises. On the other hand, the increase of labor cost caused by excessive social

Table 3.2 Social insurance contributions of some countries: %

Country	Pension insurance	Medical treatment and Maternal	Unemployment	Industrial injury	Total contribution rate
Germany	9.40	7.30	1.50	1.00–5.00	19.20–23.20
USA	6.20	1.45	6.00	1.34	14.99
Japan	8.91	5.00	0.70–0.90	0.25–8.80	14.80–23.60
Sweden	10.21	7.45	2.91	0.30	20.90
Chile	0.00	0.00	2.40	0.95–6.80	3.40–9.20
China	18.81	8.76	0.58	0.20–1.90	28.35–30.05

Note The rest of China's insurance rate data are based on the average value of 2018 provincial capital data, except that the industrial injury insurance rate directly uses the floating interval data of the whole country. The other countries' rate data are cited from the study of Wei Shengmin and Xiang Jing (2018)

[5]Quoted from the National Development and Reform Commission website report. Web site: http://tgs.ndrc.gov.cn/jjgg/cwjd/201609/t20160908_818063.html.

insurance contribution rate is not conducive to the increase of employment, and then it will restrain the growth of investment demand and the expansion of employment. In addition, excessive social insurance contribution rate will also worsen the investment environment and reduce the attractiveness of domestic and foreign capital to invest in China.

Therefore, it is important to reduce the social insurance contribution rate and establish a more fair and reasonable determination mechanism of social insurance contribution rate, in order to lighten the burden of enterprises, to control the excessive increase of labor cost, and to promote the optimization of the allocation of labor resource. It is also an effective mean to promote enterprises to expand their investment in innovation and enhance their long-term competitiveness. At the same time, appropriately lowering social insurance contribution rate of enterprises and individuals will also stimulate enterprises to expand employment, promote the reform of enterprise income distribution, which will provide a new opportunity for improving the income of the employees.

3.2 Two Scenarios to Reduce Social Insurance Rate

In order to simplify the analysis, the research team will start with the pension insurance to design the simulation scenarios. Since the implementation of the Social insurance Law of the People's Republic of China in 2011, the number of participants in pension insurance has rapidly increased from 616 million to 942 million during 2011–2018, increasing by 53.0%. At the same time, the pension insurance contribution per participant has shown a rapid upward trend: from 2770.5 yuan in 2012 to 5727.5 yuan in 2018 (Fig. 3.5), and its growth rate was 14.4, 14.1, 19.0 and 12.5% during the last four years.

In the past few years, the rapid expansion of China's pension insurance revenue is not only reflected in the rapid increase in the number of participants after the social insurance legislation, but also reflected in the more rapid growth of the basic pension insurance contribution per participant. In view of the fact that both economic growth and price levels have remained at a relatively low level during the same period, we claim that the basic pension insurance contribution borne by enterprises and individuals have actually increased sharply in recent years.[6]

In order to simulate the macro-economic effects of reducing the social insurance contribution rate, the research team conducted the following counterfactual hypothe-

[6]According to data from the Social Security Fund released by the Ministry of Finance, fiscal subsidy income from basic pension income has risen sharply in recent years, from 284.99 billion yuan in 2011 to 727.432 billion in 2017. However, on the one hand, the proportion of financial subsidy to total pension insurance income is still small, which is not enough to change the trend of increasing burden of pension insurance for enterprises and individuals. On the other hand, even financial subsidies will eventually end up in corporate and personal taxes and fees. Therefore, from the broad sense of tax burden, the increase of financial subsidies also represents the increase of tax burden of enterprises and individuals.

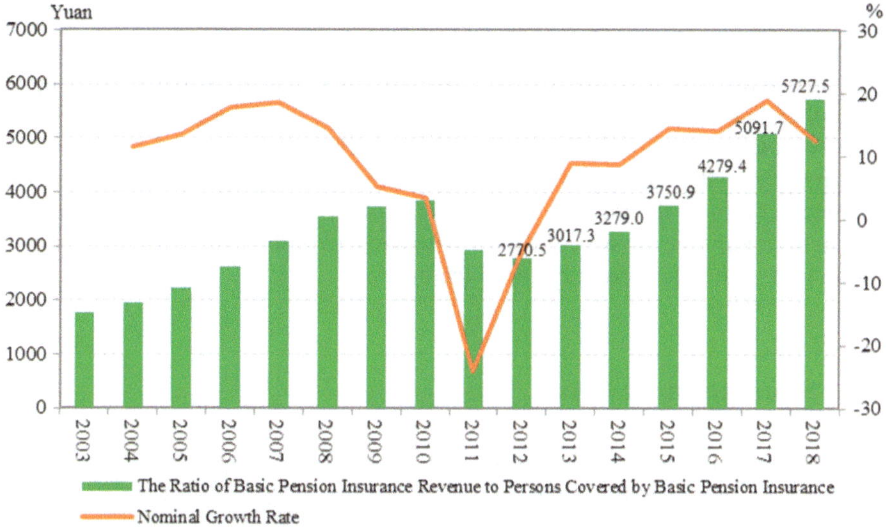

Fig. 3.5 The pension insurance revenue per participant. *Source* CEIC

ses: assuming that the pension insurance revenue per participant is assumed to be the same as in 2015, 2016 and 2017. Though the true values were 3750.9, 4279.4 and 5727.5 yuan during the three years. Under this assumption, the enterprises and individuals can reduce their social insurance payment by 469.125 and 1227.47 billion yuan 2016 and 2017, respectively, which is equivalent to 1.5 and 4.5% points reduction of insurance rate, respectively.

Coincidentally, the reduction in pension insurance payment in the two years was equal to the total tax cuts announced in 2016 and 2017 (1619.6 billion yuan). In other words, during the two years, the tax cuts were offset by the increase of social insurance contribution rate. As a result, the broad tax burden costs borne by enterprises almost haven't change. If the pension insurance payment in 2018 remains at the level of 2015(3750.9 yuan), then the enterprises and individuals can reduce their social insurance payment by 1.8 trillion yuan, which was greater than the total tax reduction of 1.3 trillion yuan in 2018.

Based on the above analysis, the research team sets up two scenarios for simulation analysis: one is to transfer the reduction of social insurance revenue to the enterprises as their profits (**scenario one**). The second is to transfer to the residents as their labor remuneration (**scenario two**).

The mechanism of the model works as follows[7]: the increase of enterprise profits will promote the growth of enterprise self-financing investment, drive the economic growth, and then promote the growth of fiscal revenue, which can partly make up for the further reduction of social insurance revenue. The increase of enterprise profit will also promote the level of employment, expand R&D investment, and play a positive role in the growth of potential output. The increase of labor compensation is more inclined to promote the increase of resident income, to promote the consumption of residents, to improve the structure of total demand, to promote the economic growth, and to lead to the increase of financial income.[8]

3.3 Simulation Results

The simulation results based on the CQMM model show that.

First, in both scenarios, GDP growth in 2016 and 2017 would have increased slightly. Under Scenario one, the GDP growth rate would have increased by 0.39 and 0.05% points over the baseline, respectively. Under scenario two, the GDP growth rate would have increased by 0.32 and 0.48% points over the baseline, respectively (Fig. 3.6). The increase in economic growth under scenario two would have been more sustainable and the magnitude of the increase will be even greater.

Secondly, the growth rate of resident consumption in both scenarios can increase slightly, and it would have been faster in scenario two than that in scenario one in 2016 and 2017. Under scenario two, it would have reached 9.61 and 8.16% respectively in the two years, which were 0.67 and 1.35% points higher than the those of scenario one (Fig. 3.7), and 0.99 and 1.47% points higher than those of the baseline. This shows that the transfer the reduction of social insurance revenue to residents as a labor compensation would have been more conducive to the increase of consumption.

Third, the urban fixed asset investment would have grown by 11.64% in 2016 under scenario one, 2.84% points higher than in scenario two, 3.33% points higher than the baseline. In 2017, due to the high base effect of the previous year, the growth of the urban fixed asset investment would have fell to 5.33% under scenario one, 1.47% points lower than in scenario two (Fig. 3.8), and 0.67% points less than the baseline. Therefore, if the reduction of social insurance revenue was transferred to the enterprises, the investment growth effect would been short, and the growth rate

[7]First, the hypothesis of this anti-fact analysis is only set for the purpose of empirical research to study the effects of reducing the burden of social enterprises or increasing employee's compensation on macro- economy. Second, before applying the CQMM model to analyze, the research team used the quarter data of social security fund income in 2016 and 2017 to interpolate the quarterly data of premium deduction; Third, the CQMM model consists of demand and supply, which can be used to analyze the adjustment of taxes and fees on employment, labor compensation, profits, material capital, potential output, economic growth, taxation, investment, consumption, imports and exports, and prices.

[8]The influence of adjusting social security rate on consumption and saving behavior of urban residents can be found in Gong Min and Yang Yan (2014).

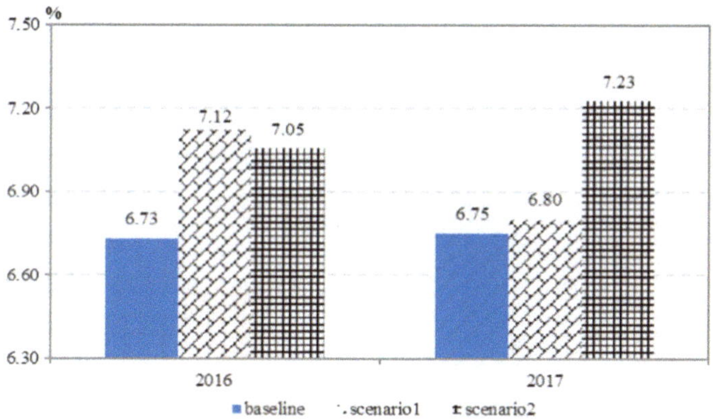

Note: Baseline represents the baseline predictive value, scenario1 represents the predicted value under simulated scenario one, and Scenario2 represents the simulated value for scenario two.

Fig. 3.6 Comparison of GDP growth. *Source* Calculated by the research team

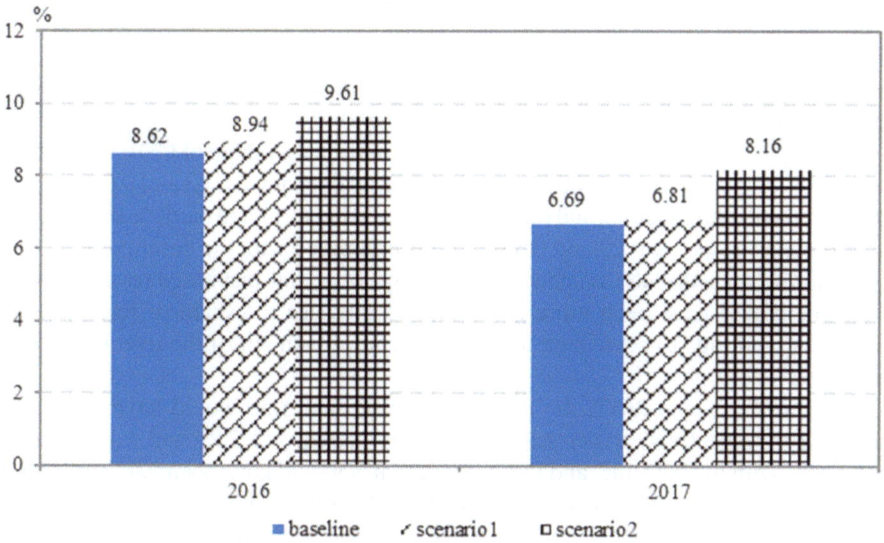

Fig. 3.7 Consumption growth rate of comparable price residents. *Source* Calculated by the research team

of investment would have fluctuated compared with scenario two. If the reduction of social insurance revenue was transferred to the residents, then the growth would have been sustainable. The growth rate of total capital formation under both scenarios also would have appeared a similar situation. Under scenario one, the total capital formation growth rate would have reached 6.83% in 2016, up 0.66% points compared with scenario two, up 0.55% points compared with the baseline. In 2017, the situation reversed under scenario one, the total capital formation growth rate would have been

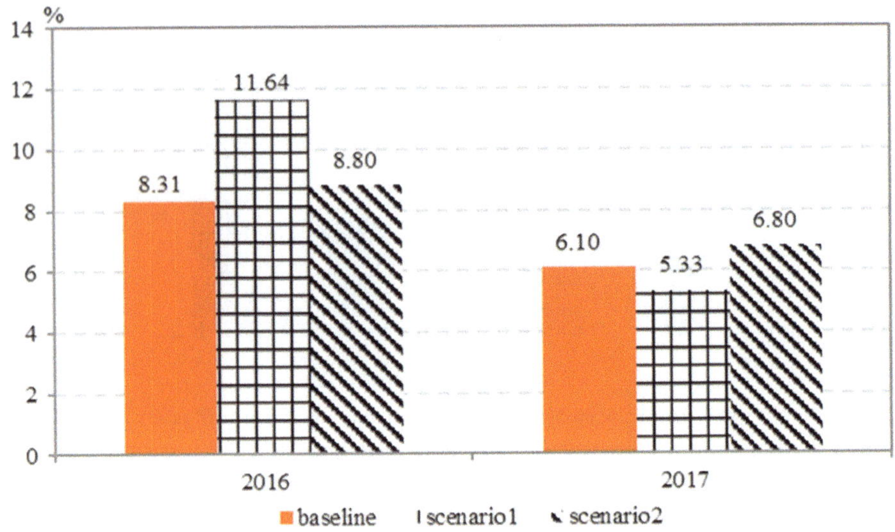

Fig. 3.8 Fixed asset investment growth rate in urban. *Source* Calculated by the research team

4.46%, roughly the same as under scenario two, down 0.25% points compared with the baseline.

Fourth, in 2016 and 2017, the resident consumption as a share of GDP would have been 37.91 and 37.92% respectively under scenario one, down 0.03 and 0.01% points compared with the baseline, and these shares would be 38.17 and 38.50% respectively under scenario two, up 0.23 and 0.58% points compared with the baseline (Fig. 3.9).

It can be seen that the transfer the reduction of social insurance revenue to the residents would have been more conducive to increase the share of resident consumption, and thus to contribute to the further improvement of the overall demand structure.

Fifth, in 2016 and 2017, the fiscal revenue growth rate would have been 7.02 and 9.21% respectively under scenario one, an increase of 2.29 and 1.14% points compared with the baseline. and these growth rates would have been 5.48 and 9.41% respectively under scenario two, up 0.75 and 1.34% points compared with the baseline (Fig. 3.10). It can be seen that the transfer of the reduction of social insurance revenue to enterprises would have been more conducive to the growth of fiscal revenue in the short term, but the transfer to the residents would have produced a more sustainable fiscal revenue growth. However, on the whole, the increase in revenue growth under the circumstances of increasing profits of enterprises is still greater than that of increasing the income of residents. Therefore, from the perspective of policy feasibility, the former has more advantages in ensuring the financial subsidies, and hence avoiding the short-term welfare decline of the insured.

Finally, from the perspective of employment, a positive employment growth effect appears in the both scenarios, although the effect is relatively small. In 2016 and 2017, the employment growth rate would have been 0.01 and 0.02% points higher than the

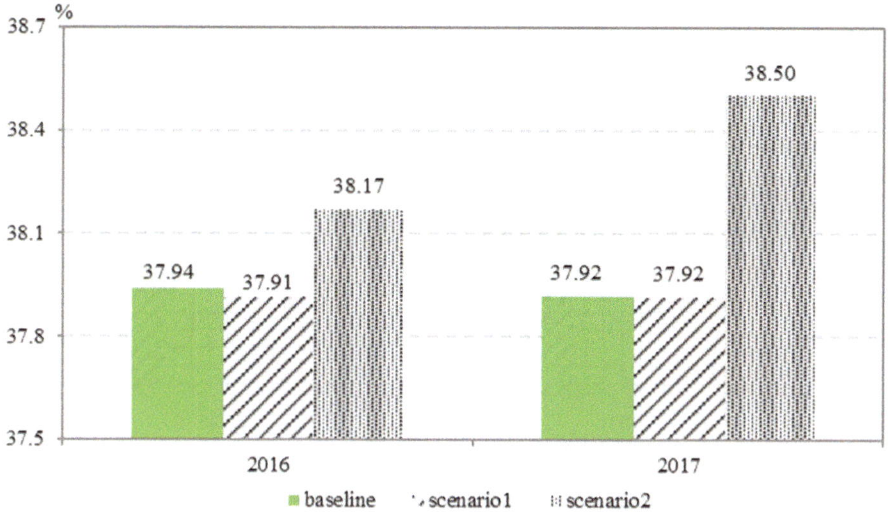

Fig. 3.9 Resident consumption ratio under expenditure method. *Source* Calculated by the research team

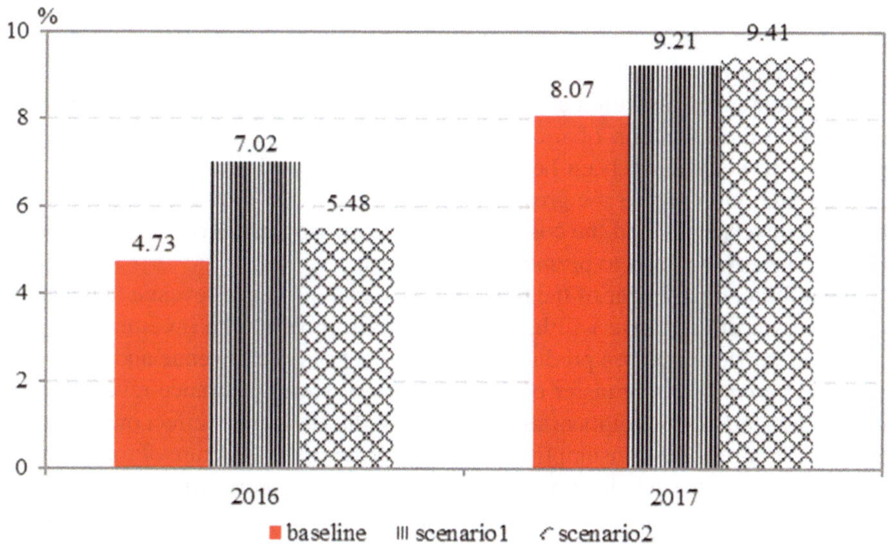

Fig. 3.10 Growth rate of fiscal revenue. *Source* Calculated by the research team

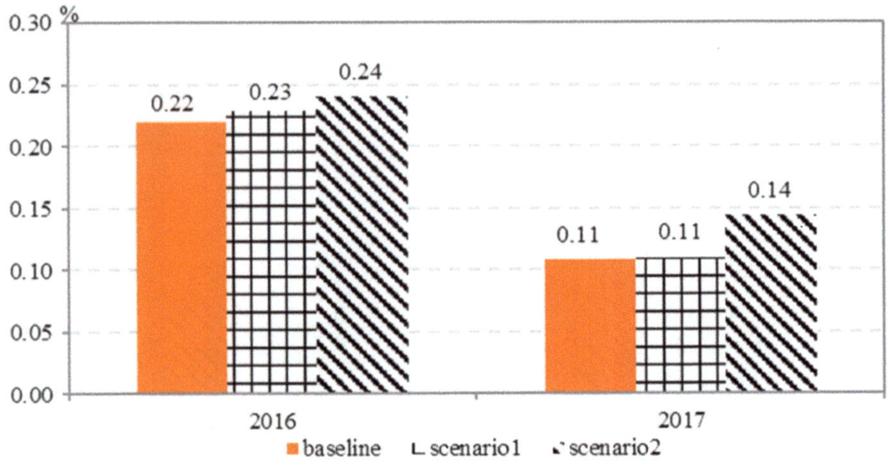

Fig. 3.11 Growth rate of employment. *Source* Calculated by the research team

baseline under scenario one, respectively. The employment growth was roughly the same as the baseline in 2016, and 0.03% points higher than the baseline in 2017 (Fig. 3.11) under scenario two. Therefore, on the whole, the employment effects of the two scenarios are basically the same.

To sum up, the simulation analysis based on CQMM model shows that whether transferring the reduction of social insurance revenue to the enterprises or to the residents, it would have been helpful to economic growth, to the growth of resident consumption and to the growth of fiscal revenue. At the same time, it would have effectively lightened the cost burden of enterprises, encouraged enterprises to increase investment, and to promote employment.

In addition, the transfer of the reduction of social insurance revenue to the enterprise as its profit increase will be more helpful to promote the investment growth of the enterprises, and then produce a greater effect of fiscal revenue and short-term economic growth. The transfer of the reduction of social insurance revenue to the residents as their labor compensation would have had a stronger effect on promoting the growth of resident consumption, and on improving the structure of total demand and on realizing the rebalancing adjustment of the economic structure. Therefore, from the perspective of high-quality growth, the transfer of the reduction of social insurance revenue to the residents would have been better policy effect.

Chapter 4
Policy Recommendations

In 2018, as the economy achieved stable growth, the economic structure continued to optimize, the employment situation remained stable, the key tasks of "three cuts, one reduction, one complement"[1] were firmly advanced, and the assets-liability ratio of enterprises, especially those controlled by the state, continued to decline.

At the same time, the downward pressure on economic growth was also growing.

First, fixed asset investment growth rate continues to decline. In the next two years, the weakening of the global economic expansion and the uncertainty of China and the United States trade frictions will put a greater downward pressure on China's export-oriented investment growth in the manufacturing sector. It is also likely to reverse the recovery growth that has begun in private and manufacturing investment since 2017.

Second, per capita consumer spending growth is difficult to rebound quickly. With acceleration of population aging, the growth rate of labor productivity in China has also slowed down in recent years. With the sharp rise of household debt ratio in the past two years, the growth rate of household consumption expenditure will be hard to increase rapidly.

Finally, the investment of new RMB loans constituted a serious distortion and needs to be adjusted. While credit volumes have expanded tremendously over the past three years, the proportion of loans invested in the real economy has fallen sharply to 50%, and loans to real estate and households both have risen sharply. This not only reduces the efficiency of the use of credit resources, but also inhibits the expansion of the investment demand of the real economy, aggravates the bubble of the real estate market, and then increases the systemic risk of the financial system.

Forecast based on CQMM model shows that China's economic growth will continue to slowdown in the next two years. If China and the United States successfully reach a trade agreement, then real GDP is expected to grow by 6.4% in 2019, 0.2% points lower than in 2018. If China and the United States fail to reach a trade agreement in 2019, then the GDP growth will be reduced by 0.16% points.

[1]Supply-side structural reform: Cutting overcapacity, de-stocking, de-leveraging, reducing costs and -improving underdeveloped areas.

China's Macroeconomic Outlook, Current Chinese Economic Report Series,
https://doi.org/10.1007/978-981-13-9357-0_4

In terms of investment, although the slowdown in global economic expansion in the next two years will dampen the growth of export-oriented manufacturing investment, the new round of infrastructure investment expansion initiated since the end of 2018 and the robust and positive monetary policy of 2019 will largely reverse the declining trend in investment growth if China and the United States succeed in reaching a trade agreement. Non-state-owned investment will grow at a slow pace in the next two years, and growth is unlikely to rebound quickly. Fixed asset investment (excluding farmers) is expected to grow 7.25%, up 1.23% points over 2018. State-owned investment is expected to grow 7.21%, while non-state investment is expected to grow 7.42%.

In terms of consumption, the growth rate of real income of residents in the next two years will continue to be stable with a slight decline, and the household debt ratio has risen rapidly in recent years. In 2019, the per capita real disposable income of urban residents is expected to increase by 6.03%, an increase of only 0.43% points over 2018, while the per capita cash income for rural residents is expected to rise 8.16%, down 1.75% points over 2018. The retail sales of consumer goods are expected to grow 8.92% in nominal terms in 2019, down 0.13% points over 2018.

Why has the downward pressure on China's economy persisted over the last decade? The essential issue is that the pattern of investment-driven growth has not yet to be reversed.

After 2015, the decline in private investment growth directly dampened the growth in manufacturing investment, which in turn led to a decline in industrial value-added growth. From the perspective of steady investment, in order to offset the decline in the growth rate of non-governmental investment, governments at all levels have to expand their investment in infrastructure, and strengthen the state-owned investment in the relevant monopolistic fields (including real estate). This directly raised the debt ratio of governments and state-owned enterprises. From the point of view of fiscal revenue, the decline in the growth of industrial value added directly restrains the growth of government revenue, increases the dependence of local governments on land transfer income, and thus fosters the bubble of the real estate market. From the point of view of the allocation of credit resources, the decline of profit margin in manufacturing and the rising debt ratio of enterprises lead to the difficulty of credit resources entering the real economy. Expanded credit was either idle within the financial system, or sucked into the real estate sector and lent to the residential sector, leading to a sharp rise in household debt ratio. The increase in household debt ratio has begun to restrain the growth of consumer spending when the real income growth rate is difficult to increase rapidly. Since the existing investment-driven growth pattern has not completely changed, if the growth rate of non-governmental investment could not rebound rapidly, then the cycle of "stable growth", "broad credit", "highly leverage of the local governments, of the state-owned and of the real estate companies", "household high debt ratios", "tight credit, financial consolidation" and "slower growth" would be hard to crack.

Moreover, if the growth rate of non-governmental investment does not rebound quickly in a long period of time, it will not be conducive to the adjustment of the economic structure and the promotion of economic benefits. First, the decline in private investment growth will directly curb the expansion and upgrading of the industry, especially manufacturing. Second, the decline in private investment growth will distort the investment structure. In recent years, for the purpose of stable investment, China's total investment in manufacturing investment has continued to decline, infrastructure investment and investment in real estate continue to increase and maintain a high proportion. Such an investment structure will not only reduce investment efficiency, but also increase the fragility of the financial system. Finally, in order to reverse the declining trend in labor productivity growth, China must rely on the rapid increase of manufacturing labor productivity. Effective investment expansion (especially private investment) is necessary to accelerate labor productivity growth by promoting the transformation and upgrading of manufacturing industry.

Therefore, in 2019, in order to break this cycle, the central government has issued policies, through financial support, tax cuts, comprehensive support for private enterprises financing, to ensure a sustained, stable and rapid growth of private investment.

Considering that the weakening of the global economic expansion in the next two years will continue to restrain the growth of manufacturing exports and profits, the research team proposes that while continuing to implement a large-scale inclusive tax cut policy, social insurance contribution rate should also be appropriately reduced. China should effectively lighten the burden of enterprises, reduce the cost of enterprises, promote the effective investment growth of enterprises, enhance the competitiveness of enterprises, and achieve stable investment and stable employment.

First of all, reducing the social insurance contribution rate is beneficial to the increase of enterprise profit, which can promote the investment growth of enterprises, drive the economic growth, and then improve the growth rate of financial revenue. Secondly, reducing the cost of labor is also beneficial to the expansion of employment, to the increase of resident income, to the increase of resident consumption, and to the improvement of the structure of total demand. Finally, the decrease of enterprise burden and the increase of profit growth will benefit the growth of R&D investment, and then promote the technological progress and labor productivity.

In recent years, with the acceleration of the population aging, the average pension insurance contribution per participant in China has increased rapidly. Under the existing social insurance contribution system, the social insurance burden that enterprises and individuals have to bear is also increasing rapidly. In order to simulate the macro-economic effects of reducing social insurance contribution rate, the research team conducts some counterfactual analysis assumptions: assuming that the pension insurance contribution per participant is assumed to remain at 3750.9 yuan in 2015, 2016 and 2017, though the true premium were 3750.9, 4279.4 and 5727.5 yuan in the three years respectively. Under this assumption, the burden of businesses or individuals in 2016 and 2017 will be reduced by 469.125 billion yuan and 1227.47 billion yuan, respectively. On this basis, the research team sets up two simulation scenarios: one is to transfer all of the reduced social insurance revenue (469.125 and 1227.47 billion yuan) to the enterprises as their profit (scenario one).The second is to transfer all of the reduced social insurance revenue to the residents as their labor remuneration (scenario two).

Based on the simulation analysis of CQMM model, it is found that whether the reduction of social insurance contribution was the transferred to enterprises or residents, it would help promote economic growth, and promote the growth of resident consumption and promote the growth of fiscal revenue. At the same time, because it can effectively lighten the burden of enterprises, it can also encourage enterprises to increase investment, and then promote employment and increase resident income.

In addition, the transfer of the reduction of social insurance revenue to the enterprises will be more helpful to promote the investment growth of the enterprises, and then produce a greater effect of fiscal revenue and economic growth in short-term. The transfer of reduction of social insurance revenue to the residents would have a stronger effect on promoting the growth of resident consumption, and can further improve the structure of total demand and realize the rebalancing adjustment of the economic structure in long-term. Therefore, from the perspective of high-quality growth, the transfer of reduction of social insurance revenue to the residents would have a better policy effect.

Overall, export-oriented manufacturing investment growth will face greater downward pressure in the next two years, as global economic expansion slows down. The model forecasts that non-state-owned investment will continue to grow at a slow pace in the next two years, and that the pace of growth is difficult to rebound quickly. Since the existing investment-driven growth pattern has not completely changed, if the growth rate of non-governmental investment could not rebound rapidly, then the cycle of "stable growth", "broad credit", "highly leverage of the local governments, of the state-owned and of the real estate companies", "household high debt ratios", "tight credit, financial consolidation" and "slower growth" would be hard to crack.

At present, the central government has issued a series of policies, such as tax cuts, to fully support the private enterprises to ensure a sustained, stable and rapid growth of private investment. These policies certainly caught the crux of the problem, and found a breakthrough to solve the above policy implementation difficulties.

In this regard, we put forward the following policy recommendations:

First, to achieve the short-term goal—stable investment, as well as to achieve the long-term goal—enhance the competitiveness of enterprises, China should fully support private enterprise financing. The current policies, such as tax cuts and fee reduction, should focus on crowding out inefficient investment, promoting effective investment growth, encouraging enterprises to increase investment in R&D, enhancing competitiveness, and promoting the transformation and upgrading of industries, in order to achieve sustained and rapid labor productivity growth.

Secondly, monetary policy should maintain reasonably sufficient liquidity while controlling the total amount, and provide conditions for stable and effective investment growth. While maintaining a reasonable increase in the credit volume and social financing in the broad sense of money M2, emphasis should be placed on adjusting the credit structure to ensure that the share of loans to real economy is stable at more than 60%, in order to truly implement the goal of the real economy of financial services. At the same time, the ability and willingness of finance to serve the real economy should be improved through mechanism innovation.

Third, China's government revenue consists of four parts, namely, general public budget revenue, government fund revenue, social insurance fund revenue and state-owned capital operating budget revenue. In 2017, China's broad-based government revenue as a share of GDP was 34.4, 3.2% points higher than that of the United States, 2.4% points higher than the average of the emerging and developing economies, and just 4.3% points lower than the average of advanced economies. Therefore, we should continue to implement a large-scale inclusive policy to reduce the macro-tax burden.

Fourthly, the indirect tax, such as value added tax and consumption tax, is the main body of taxation. Though it is possible theoretically for enterprises to transfer the indirect tax burden to consumers, the tax transfer ability of enterprises is very limited, because of the weak demand at home and abroad and relative excess capacity. As a result of "replacing business tax with VAT", many small and medium-sized enterprises (mostly private enterprises) have failed to obtain the policy dividend of reducing the tax burden, due to financial supervision and the tax regulatory system. Worsen, they were forced to bear an increase in the actual tax burden. The reform of social insurance contribution to the full responsibility of the state tax authorities means the strengthening of the supervision of social insurance funds, the direct result of which is that small and medium-sized enterprises, which were previously relatively weak in terms of payment and compliance of social insurance funds, are facing further hardship in their operating costs. Therefore, in order to promote the development of small and medium-sized enterprises and realize the steady growth of employment, China should not only strengthen the compliance of social insurance contributions, but also reduce the social insurance rate properly, lighten the burden of enterprises in order to promote the development of small and medium enterprises.

Fifth, China should be very vigilant against the negative impact of the rapid rise of household debt ratio on the growth of consumer expenditure. With the acceleration of the population aging, the social insurance system has not yet been perfected, and the income gap between the urban and the rural is still severe, what is more important, in a situation where the real income growth of residents is slowed down because of low growth rate of labor productivity, and it is difficult to increase rapidly. The rapid increase of household debt ratio will restrain the growth of resident consumption expenditure and hinder the transformation of economic growth mode.

Appendix A
A Questionnaire Report on China's Macroeconomy and Policy

In order to grasp China's macroeconomic situation and policy trends in a timely manner, Economic Information Daily of Xinhua News Agency and the Center for Macroeconomic Research at Xiamen University[1] jointly carried out a twice-yearly "questionnaire survey on China's economic situation and policy" since August 2013.

This is the 12th survey. The questionnaire designed 18 questions directly related to the current macroeconomic operation and policy trends in China. In January 2019, we sent e-mail invitations to economists in relevant fields. A valid response was received from 127 experts. Through this questionnaire survey, we have obtained the latest professional understanding and expectations on the world economic situation, and the economic situation of China in 2019. The results of this questionnaire are as follows:

A.1 The World Economic Situation in 2019

According to the latest forecast of the of the International Monetary Fund (IMF) on 21 January 2019, the United States economic growth rate in 2019 was 2.5, 0.4% points lower than that in 2018, and it is in line with its October 2018 forecast. With regard to growth rate the United States economy in 2019, 10% of the experts expected that the economic growth rate of USA would be between 1.5 and 2.0%; 67% expected between 2.1 and 2.5%; 22% expected between 2.6 and 3.0%; 1% expected between 3.1 and 3.5%. Overall, more than 90% of the experts expected that the US economy would grow slower in 2019 than in 2018.

[1]One of the Key Research Institutes of Humanities and Social Sciences of the Ministry of Education of China.

China's Macroeconomic Outlook, Current Chinese Economic Report Series,
https://doi.org/10.1007/978-981-13-9357-0

According to the latest forecast of the IMF on January 21, 2019, the GDP growth rate of the Eurozone in 2019 is 1.6%, which is 0.2% points lower than that of 2018. The forecast is also down 0.3% points from its October 2018 forecast. With regard the economic growth rate of Eurozone in 2019, 2% of the experts expected that the economic growth rate of Eurozone would be below 1.2% in 2019; 69% expected between 1.3 and 1.5%; 22% expected between 1.6 and 1.8%; 1% expected 1.9 and 2.1%. Overall, almost all of the experts believed that the economy would grow slower in 2019 than in 2018.

As of December 31, 2018, the Euro exchange rate against the US dollar was 1.1453, higher than the average of the first four months of 2018. In 2019, the process of Brexit and the increase in economic uncertainty in the Eurozone could make a strong Euro unsustainable. With regard to the Euro exchange rate against the US dollar at the end of 2019, 54% of experts expect the Euro to remain stable against the dollar; 32% of the experts expected that the Euro would depreciate, and Euro exchange rate would be between 1.0 and 1.13; 14% of the experts expected the Euro exchange rate would be between 1.14 and 1.33. Overall, more than half of experts believe the Euro is stable against the dollar, but more than 30% believe the Euro will continue to depreciate against the dollar in 2019.

A.2 The China's Economic Situation in 2019

China's GDP grew 6.6% in 2018, down 0.2% over the previous year, according to the data released by the National Bureau of Statistics on Jan. 21, 2019. With regard to China's GDP growth rate in 2019, only 1% of experts expected that it would be between 6.5 and 6.8%; 51% expected 6.3 and 6.5%; 38% expected between 6.1 and 6.3%. 5% of the experts expected it would be below 6%. Overall, more than 90% of experts believe that China's GDP growth rate in 2019 will be lower than in 2018.

In 2018, China's Consumer Price (CPI) was 2.1%, an increase of 0.5% points over the previous year. Core CPI, which excludes food and energy prices, was 1.9%, down 0.3% points over the previous year. With regard to the trend of CPI in 2019, 1% of the experts expected it to be more than 3.1%; 10% of experts expected it to be between 2.6 and 3.0%; 45% of experts expected it to be between 2.1 and 2.5%; 42% expected it to be between 1.6 and 2.0%; 2% of the experts expected to be below 1.5%. Overall, nearly 60% of experts believe CPI would increase in 2019, and more than 40% expected it will be lower than in 2018.

China's Producer Price Index (PPI) was 3.5% in 2018, down 2.8% points over the previous year. With regard to China's PPI in 2019, 1% of the experts expected it to be between 5.0 and 6.0%; 68% expected between 3.0 and 4.0%; 29% expected between 2.0 and 3.0%; 2% expected it to be below 0%. Overall, almost all experts expected PPI to be below 4.0% in 2019.

Fixed asset investment (excluding farmers) increased 5.9% in 2018, down 1.3% points over the previous year. Among them, investment in manufacturing industry increased 9.5%, up 4.7% points over the previous year, while investment in real estate increased 9.5%, an increase of 5.9% points over the previous year. Infrastructure investment grew 3.8%, down 16.2% points over the previous year.

(1) With regard to the growth rate in fixed asset investment in 2019, 2% of experts expected to be between 2.0 and 4.0%; 48% between 4.0 and 6.0%; 42% expected between 6.0 and 8.0%; 6% expected be between 8.0 and 10.0; 2% expected to exceed 10%.
(2) With regard to the growth rate of the manufacturing investment in 2019, 13% of experts believed that it would continue to accelerate; 48% of the experts believed that the investment in manufacturing remained basically stable; 39% of the experts expected it would slow down.
(3) With regard to the growth rate of real estate investment in 2019, 60% of experts expected it to slow down; 30% of experts believed it to be stable, and 10% of experts expected it to continue to accelerate.
(4) With regard to the growth rate of infrastructure investment in 2019, 60% of experts expected it will continue to accelerate; 28% of experts expected it to be stable; 12% expected it to slow down.

Overall, compared with the previous year, half of experts expect growth rate of fixed asset investment will be higher in 2019. Nearly half of experts expected the growth rate of manufacturing investment to remain stable in 2019; nearly 40% also expect investment growth to slow down; 60% of experts expected real estate investment to slow down; and 60% of the experts expected infrastructure investment to continue to accelerate.

In 2018, investment by state-owned and state-controlled enterprises grew 1.9%, down 8.2% points over the previous year. Private investment grew 8.7%, up 2.7% over the previous year. Private investment accounted for 62.0% of the total investment, an increase of 1.6% points over last year.

(1) With regard to the growth rate of the investment of state-owned and state-controlled enterprises in 2019, 1% of the experts expected it to be less than 0%; 79% of experts expected between 1.0 and 5.0%; 14% expected between 5.0 and 8.0%; 5% expected between 8.0–10.0%; 1% expected it to be higher than 10.0%.
(2) With regard to the growth rate of the private investment in 2019, 7% of the experts expected it to be less than 5%; 47% of the experts expected 5.0 and 8.0%; 40 expected between 8.0 and 10%; and 4% expected 10.0 and 12.0%; 2% expected above 12%.

Retail sales of consumer goods rose 9.0% in nominal terms in 2018, down 1.2% points over the previous year. With regard to the growth rate of retail sales of consumer goods in 2019, 57% of experts expected it to be between 8.5 and 8.9%; 26% expected 9.0 and 9.4%; 10% expected it to be below 8.4%; 5% believed it to be between 9.5 and 9.9%; 2% believed it to be above 10%. Overall, 67% of experts believed that the it would be lower than in 2018.

In 2018, China's exports of goods totaled 16417.7 billion yuan, and it rose 7.1, down 3.7% points over the previous year. As for the growth rate of the total exports in 2019, 64% of the experts expected it to be between 5.1 and 7.0%; 18% expected it to be below 5.0%; 15% expected it to be between 7.1 and 9.0%; only 3% believed it to be between 9.1 and 11.0%. Overall, more than 80% of the experts expected it to slowdown compared with 2018.

China's imports of goods totaled 14087.4 billion yuan in 2018, and the growth rate was 12.9%, down 5.8% points over the previous year. With regard to growth rate of the total imports in 2019, 39% of the experts expected it to be between 10.0 and 12.0%; 35% expected between 12.0 and 14.0%; 15% expected it to be below 10%;10% expected it to be between 14.0 and 16.0%; only 1% expected it to exceed 16%. Overall, more than 60% of the experts expected it to be more than in 2018.

Since 2018, the rise in U.S. interest rates and the continued rise in the dollar index have caused the yuan to fluctuate sharply against the dollar. As of December 31, 2018, the median exchange rate of the RMB against the US dollar was 6.8755. Regarding to the exchange rate at the end of 2019, 45% of the experts expected the RMB to remain stable against the US dollar; 40% expected the RMB to continue to depreciate, with a mid-point of between 6.9 and 7.3 yuan; 15% expected the RMB would appreciated, with a mid-point between 6.5 and 6.85 yuan. Overall, more than 40% of experts believed the RMB remained stable, while 40% believed they would depreciate.

A.3 The Forecast of China's Macro-Economic Policy in 2019

At the end of December 2018, China's M2 balance was 182.67 trillion yuan. The growth rate of M2 balance was 8.1%, which was the same compared with December of previous year, though it was 0.1% points higher than at the end of November of 2018. Regarding to the growth rate of M2 growth in 2019, 6% expected it to be below 7.4%; 23% expected it to be between 7.5 and 8.0%; 51% of experts expected 8.1 and 8.6%; 19% expected 8.7 and 9.2%; 1% expected it to be above 9.3%. Overall, more than 70% of experts believed that China's M2 growth rate in 2019 will be higher than in 2018. Most experts believe the Chinese government will continue to adopt a moderately neutral monetary policy in 2019.

The 2018 Central Economic work Conference clearly pointed out that macro-policy should strengthen counter-cyclical adjustment, prudent monetary policy should be loosened, sufficient liquidity should be maintained reasonably, and monetary policy transmission mechanism should be improved. So, what will be the policy options for China's monetary authority in 2019? The multiple choice survey show that 73% of the experts chose "maintain reasonable liquidity and adequate market interest rates, encourage financial institutions to increase their support for the real economy, and promote the reasonable growth of monetary credit and social financing"; 68% of experts chose "continue to use policy tools to further improve private financial services enterprises, such as reduction of reserve requirement ratio, targeted at private, small and micro enterprises"; 64% of experts chose "continue to use the combination of monetary policy tools, strengthen policy communication and coordination, balance the relationship between aggregate and structure, and consolidate the micro-foundation of policy transmission"; 57% of experts chose "according to the principles of marketization and rule of law, we should give full play to the role of credit, bonds and equity, and actively support private enterprise bond financing and equity financing instruments"; 56% of experts chose "Continue to reduce reserve ratio, reduce open market operations in the money market, reduce financing costs, repair market distortions, maintain reasonable and adequate liquidity, and effectively ease the transmission mechanism of monetary policy"; 56% of experts chose "vigorously develop the direct financing market, promote the pilot reform of the scientific innovation board and the registration system, and establish a multi-level capital market"; 48% of experts chose "innovate bank capital replenishment tools, increase the tolerance of non-performing loans, treat private enterprises and state-owned enterprises fairly, and implement inclusive finance and competition neutrality". In addition, a small number of experts have made other recommendations on the implementation of monetary policy in China, such as lower interest rates, a reasonable view of shadow banking resources allocation function to avoid the one-size-fits-all approach.

With regard to the policies to solve the problem of financing difficult financing for private enterprises, the multi-choice survey show that 74% of experts chose "reducing taxes and fees, strengthen financing guarantee, finance interest discount, optimize credit system, and reduce financing cost of private enterprises and small and micro-enterprises"; 72% chose "strengthen monetary policy support for small and medium-sized banks and further lower reservation ratio to include more small and medium-sized banks"; 72% chose "activating the capital market, restoring the financing function of the stock market, promoting the landing of the scientific innovation board and the registration system, in order to support small and micro-enterprises and innovative enterprises"; 68% chose "Give full play to the function of the main channel of credit and improve the availability of the credit financing of the private enterprises. To reform the supervision and incentive mechanism of financial institutions. Insist on the principle of market-oriented pricing, strictly abide by the risk management discipline, and provide the better financing service for the private enterprises"; 61% of experts chose "In accordance with the principles of marketization and rule of law, the people's Bank of China provides initial guiding funds, drives financial institutions and social capital to participate together, and sets up equity financing support tools for private enterprises"; 52% of the experts believed that "continue to innovate commercial bank capital replenishment tools, expand the core capital replenishment channels of small and medium-sized banks, expand the investor group, and substantially improve the capital replenishment ability of small and medium-sized banks"; 51% of experts believed that "the establishment of private enterprise bond financing support tools, by the central bank to provide part of the initial funds, through professional institutions, market-oriented operation, the sale of credit risk mitigation tools and guarantees to increase credit, and other means, to provide credit support for private enterprises to issue debt". In addition, a small number of experts made other policy recommendations on how to effectively address the difficult financing costs of private enterprises, etc.

The central government clearly pointed out that the active fiscal policy in 2019 should be more effective, implement larger-scale tax cuts and lower fees, and significantly increase the size of local government special bonds. With regard to the fiscal policy to be implemented in 2019, the multiple choice survey show that 81% of experts believe that "implement larger tax cuts, insist on a combination of inclusive tax cuts and structural tax cuts, focus on reducing the burden on manufacturing and small and micro-enterprises, and support the real economy"; 72% of experts believed that "increase reduction in fees, standardize local charges, and step up efforts to investigate and crack down on unreasonable charges"; 67% of experts believed that "improve the efficiency of the allocation of financial funds, insist on maintaining pressure, focus on key areas and weak links, and further adjust and optimize the expenditure structure, to increase investment in poverty alleviation, agriculture, rural areas, structural adjustment, scientific and technological innovation, ecological and environmental protection, and people's livelihood. Major efforts should be made to reduce general spending, eliminate inefficient and ineffective expenditures"; 60% of experts believed that "use capital expenditures for public welfare in accordance with the law, focus on supporting major national strategies, and advance major railway projects, highways, major water conservancy projects, rural revitalization, ecological and environmental protection, and urban infrastructure, public welfare infrastructure construction in rural infrastructure, etc."; 58% of experts believe that "according to the economic situation and various aspects of expenditure demand, expand the scale of fiscal expenditure., increase the size of special bonds of local governments and support the construction of major projects under construction and their deficiency"; 53% of experts believed that "in promoting structural adjustment of the economy, active fiscal policy, in addition to measures such as large-scale tax cuts and fees reduction, also needs to coordinate with monetary policy to ensure that liquidity performance truly enters the real economy, to promote the development of small and medium-sized enterprises, promote the upgrading of industrial structure adjustment"; 52% of experts believed that "improve the efficiency of the use of financial funds, better promote the policy to be effective, continue to revitalize the fiscal stock of funds, and recover all long-term precipitated funds that are difficult to spend". In addition, a small number of experts have put forward other suggestions for the implementation of China's fiscal policy.

The Central Economic Work Conference was held in Beijing from December 19–21, 2018, and it defined the key tasks for the whole year of 2019. So, what are the most prominent points? The multi-choice survey show that 67% of experts believe that "promote the high-quality development of manufacturing industry", 67% of experts believe that "promote the formation of a strong domestic market", 64% of experts believe that "promote all-round opening up to the outside world"; 60% of experts believe that "accelerate economic restructuring"; 56% believe that "improve security and improve people's livelihood"; 41% believe that the "solid promotion of rural revitalization strategy"; and 33% believe that "promote coordinated regional development". In addition, a small number of experts have put forward other views, including: greater tax cuts and fees reduction; long-term mechanisms for the development of the real estate market; strengthening the fundamental position of competition policy; and promoting green development, etc.

High-quality development and deepening reform and opening-up will be the main line of economic and social development. So, what will be the focus of the China's macro-policy in the next phase? The multi-choice survey show that 82% of experts believe that "in-depth promotion of supply-side structural reform, speeding up the construction of a modern economic system, strengthening the protection of intellectual property rights, so that innovation becomes the first driving force for development"; 82% of experts believe that "stabilize the investment environment, increase opening up to the outside world, relax market access, protect the legitimate rights and interests of foreign-funded enterprises in China, provide better services for enterprises from all over the world to invest in China, and promote the in-depth development of joint construction of Belt and Road"; 69% of experts believe that "through vigorously developing the service industry to increase employment, ensure stable growth in basic expenditure on people's livelihood, such as wages, education, social insurance, and so on, strengthen the work of eradicating poverty and reducing the income gap"; 63% of experts believe that "maintain steady and healthy economic development, adhere to the implementation of positive fiscal policy and prudent monetary policy, improve the forward-looking, flexibility, effectiveness of the policy"; 50% of experts believe that "implementation of rural revitalization strategy and regional coordinated development strategy".

In addition, a small number of experts proposed other macro-policy priorities, including: multi-measures to stabilize consumption growth; more large-scale tax cuts and fees reduction; to ensure that investment risks are predictable, manageable and affordable; to reduce taxes on a larger scale and more significantly, and to implement inclusive tax breaks for small and micro-enterprises; to reduce the tax burden of residents, promote fair competition review, liberalize unnecessary market access restrictions, and promote consumption escalation; to deepen the opening to the outside world at a high level and promote the integration of megacities, urban agglomeration and urban belt into the international division of labor and cooperative competition system; to create a first-class international business environment, improve the level of internationalization of cities, accelerate the construction of economic canters with global influence, gather high-end global factors, high-level talent and regional headquarters and investment, and sales of multinational companies; to open the land market in an orderly manner, give farmers greater and more solid land rights and interests, launch pilot projects for market-based legalization of rural land resources, and slow down the downward pressure on the economy with the dividends of land reform, and so on.

127 experts participated in the questionnaire (ranked by name): Pak Pui-wen, Bi Jiyao, Chang Xin, Chen Changbing, Chen Gong, Chen Heng, Chen Jianbao, Chen Jinmei, Chen Kunting, Chen Longnan, Chen Lei, Chen Mengen, Chen Shou-dong, Chen Xikang, Chen Xuebin, Chen Yanbin, Chen Zhiyong, Dai Quizao,

Deng Xiang, Dong Ximiao, Dong Zhiyong, Fan Qian, Gao Bo, Gong Gang, Guo Qiyou, Guo Xibao, Guo Xiaohe, Guo Zhiyi, Han Zhaozhou, He Jingtong, Hua Yicheng, Huang Jianhui, Huang Xianfeng, Huang Zhigang, Jian Jinhan, Jian Xinhua, Jiang Yongmu, Jin Tao, Li Chunqi, Li Haizheng, Li Jianwei, Li Jun, Li Junsheng, Li Shantong, Li Xuesong, Li Yingdong, Liang Jiarui, Lin Xuegui, Liu GE, Liu Jianping, Liu Jinquan, Liu Qiuzhi, Liu Shiguo, Liu Xiaoxin, Liu Zhibiao, Ma Ying, Pang Jinyu, Peng Suling, Qu Wanwen, Ren Baoping, Ren Ruoen, Shao Yihang, Shen Guobing, Shen Lisheng, Shi Junyi, Su Jian, Sun Shaoyan, Sun Wei, Tang Jijun, Tian Ruzhu, Wang Tongsan, Wang Yida, Wang Cheng, Wang Dou, Wang Guocheng, Wang Junbo, Wang Meijin, Wang Susheng, Wang Yanxing, Wang Yuesheng, Wang Zongrun, Wen Chuanhao, Wu Huabin, Wu Xinru, Xian Guoming, Xiao Xingzhi, Xie Danyang, Xie Pan, Xu Xianxiang, Xu Yifan, Xu Bin, Xu Wenbin, Yan Ping, Yang Chengyu, Yang Cuihong, Yang Zhiyong, Yi Xianrong, Yin Xingmin, Yu Li, Yu Zuo, Yu Bin, Yuan Fuhua, Zang Xuheng, Zhang Donghui, Zhang Hongliang, Zhang Liqun, Zhang Liancheng, Zhang long, Zhang Mingzhi, Zhang Monan, Zhang Ping, Zhang Yuan, Zeng May Day, Zhao Changhui, Zhao Minghao, Zhao Xindong, Zhao Zhenquan, Zhao Zhijun, Zheng Chaoyu, Zheng Yusheng, Zhong Chunping, Zhou Bing, Zhou Liqun, Zhou Zejiong, Zhu Baohua, Zhu Jianping, Zhu Qigui.

Experts and scholars who participated in the questionnaire came from the Macroeconomic Research Department of the Development Research Center of the State Council, the Development Strategy and Regional Economic Research Department of the Development Research Center of the State Council, and the Forecasting Science Research Center of the Chinese Academy of Sciences. Institute of Finance, Chinese Academy of Social Sciences, Institute of Economics, Chinese Academy of Social Sciences, Institute of quantitative Economics and Technology Economics, Chinese Academy of Social Sciences, Institute of Financial and Strategic Studies, Chinese Academy of Social Sciences, Institute of World Economics and Politics, Chinese Academy of Social Sciences, Ministry of Commerce, Ministry of Finance, National Bureau of Statistics, International Liaison Department of the CPC Central Committee, CCTV, China International Economic Exchange Center, Economic Information Daily, Hengfeng Bank, Minsheng Bank, Contractor Bank, Export-Import Bank of China, China Banking Association, Taiwan "Chinese Academy of Research", Chinese Research Institute of Economics, etc., as well as Xiamen University, Shanghai International Economic and Trade University, Hong Kong University, Fujian Normal University, Fuzhou University, Liaoning University, Zhejiang University of Technology, Sun Yat-sen University, Zhongnan University, Northeast University of Finance and Economics, Beijing Normal University, Jilin University, Renmin University of China, Zhongnan University of Finance and Politics, Zhejiang University of Finance and Economics, Sichuan University, Peking University, Nanjing University, Shanghai University of Finance and Economics, Wuhan University, East China normal University, Jinan University, Nankai University, HK Chinese University, Hunan University, Central University of Finance and Economics, Xian Jiaotong University, Taiwan University, Northwestern University, Beijing University of Aeronautics and

Astronautics, City University of Hong Kong, Chongqing University of Commerce and Industry, Yunnan University of Finance and Economics, Shaanxi Normal University, China Europe International Business School, Fudan University, Tianjin University of Finance and Economics, Shandong University, Hong Kong Baptist University, City University of Hong Kong, Capital University of Economics and Economics, Huazhong University of Science and Technology, Anhui University of Finance and Economics, Shanghai Jiaotong University, Hong Kong University of Science and Technology, etc.

Finally, we would like to express our sincere thanks to the above experts for their warm participation and insights.

A Comparison of the forecasting results between the research team and 127 experts

Major macroeconomic indicators in 2019	By research team (%)		By experts (%)	
	Two sides reached a trade agreement	Two sides fail to reach a trade agreement	Interval	Proportion
GDP growth rate	6.4	6.24	6.3–6.5 6.1–6.3	51 38
CPI	2.01	2.01	2.1–2.5 1.6–2.0	45 42
PPI	1.40	1.40	3.0–4.0 0.0–2.0	68 29
Total export growth (current United States dollar)	4.42	2.23	5.1–7.0 Below 5.0	64 18
Total import growth (current United States dollar)	10.72	8.98	10.0–12.0 12.0–14.0 Below 10.0	39 35 15
Nominal growth rate of total retail sales of consumer goods	8.92	8.92	8.5–8.9 9.0–9.4	57 26
Fixed assets investment total nominal growth rate	7.25	6.57	4.0–6.0 6.0–8.0	48 42

Appendix B
Comments and Discussions

B.1 By Professor Gao Peiyong

Vice president, the Chinese Academy of Social Sciences; director of the Institute of Economics, Chinese Academy of Social Sciences

In China at present, the issue of tax cuts and fees reduction has been put on a higher level than ever before. However, recognizing that we are talking about tax cuts in 2019, and we are talking about tax cuts in the high-quality development phase, it is very different from the previous positions, views and methods.

First of all, we need to realize that this is a very professional work. There is at least one question that needs to be answered: when we use tax cuts and fees reduction as a means of macro-regulation and control, giving it the function of promoting China's economic growth in the new era, we need to tell the difference between policy adjustment and reform.

When it comes to macro-control, the Central Economic Work Conference mentioned: first, we must strengthen counter-cyclical adjustment, and second, we must adhere to supply-side structural reform unswervingly. As we know, these are two expressions based on different theories. Counter-cyclical adjustment originates from the macroeconomic policy arrangement based on Keynesian demand regulation theory, that is, the demand management theory. The supply-side structural reform originated from Xi Jinping's thought of socialist economy with Chinese characteristics in the new era, with the concept of "three phases superimposed",[2] the new normal of economy and high-quality development as clues since the 18th National Congress of the Communist Party of China (CPC). When two different macro-control measures are put together, we need to distinguish carefully. Whether tax cuts are placed in a series of counter-cyclical adjustments or supply-side structural reforms is a completely different course of action.

---

[2]To deal simultaneously with the slowdown in economic growth, making difficult structural adjustments, and absorbing the effects of the previous economic stimulus policies.

China's Macroeconomic Outlook, Current Chinese Economic Report Series,
https://doi.org/10.1007/978-981-13-9357-0

If we put it in a series of counter-cyclical adjustments, we can position it with a generalized tax cut and a reduction in fees. If we put it in a series of supply-side structural reforms, then we can use a structural tax cut and a reduction in fees. The inclusive and structural goals are different. The goal of general-benefit tax reduction is to expand demand and belong to counter-cyclical regulation sequence.The goal of structural tax cuts is not to expand demand, but to act as one of the supply-side structural reforms. Reducing costs is the goal of structural tax cuts. So today, when we talk about cutting taxes and reducing costs, we face coordination between two policy objectives: expanding demand and lowering costs. If it is aimed at expanding demand, then the target of reducing taxes and fees, or who can be reduced, can be enterprises, can also be individuals and families. So long as the disposable income of businesses and individuals can be increased to meet the goal of expanding demand, it is right to cut taxes and fees. If you put it in the cost-cutting series, then the tax cuts are targeted not at individuals, but at businesses, especially the real economy.

If we put it in a series of counter-cyclical adjustments, then we can position it with a generalized tax cut and a reduction in fees; if we put it in a supply-side structural reform sequence, then what taxes and fees to reduce? If it is to expand demand, then, reduce any tax and fee can. As long as taxes and fees are reduced, disposable income will increase and aggregate demand will increase. However, the macro-economic theory and the past macro-control practice tell us that we should reduce the tax and fee with the least time-delay effect, which will reduce the income tax. However, the tax reduction at this time has to be related to the cost.

Where is the cost? For an enterprise, the cost is in the price of a variety of goods and services. For example, this 5, 000-yuan watch has three elements in its price: cost, profit, and tax. Therefore, the choice of tax types involved in reducing taxes and charges at this time must be the taxes and fees that occur in the circulation link. In reality, the tax and fee that we call the turnover tax and fee, such as VAT. And then, ultimately, the aim of tax cuts has to be balanced with government spending. What is the difference between revenue and expenditure after the tax cut or the income deficit left behind? You can't cut one trillion dollars, unless you can find a substitute for $1 trillion.

Where does money come from? One is to increase the deficit, the other is simply to reduce their own spending. But, two different goals of tax cuts are operating differently. If the aim is to expand demand, then only one operation is right, that is, to increase the deficit, increase the national debt. Simultaneous tax cuts and spending cuts will result in a decline in aggregate social demand. However, if the deficit is increased and the treasury bonds are issued to make up for the deficit in tax cuts, then the pattern of resource allocation will not change. The amount of money collected from enterprises will still be collected, but the form has changed. Originally collected in the form of taxes and fees, now in the form of treasury bonds, the structure may be different.

It is necessary to pay back the money in the end. Even if government debt can never be repaid for life, interest will be paid. The central government now spends more than 500 billion yuan a year on interest, accounting for one sixth of its total expenditure of 3 trillion yuan, which you have to pay back. The interest on borrowing will undoubtedly be added to the total size of future government spending. Wool comes out of the sheep, or from enterprises and individuals from the collection. There is only one way to go, that is, by cutting government spending. Finally, there is the question of whether to cut taxes as a policy arrangement or as a reform action. Expanding demand is a policy arrangement, because expanding demand is not always expanding, not under any economic cycle conditions, only based on today's downward pressure on the economy is necessary to expand. At this time, tax cuts and fees can only be taken as policy measures. If you reduce it today, it will increase tomorrow. This year, you will return to the pattern of tax and tax burden in the next two years. For example, when we talked about the estate tax some years ago, we said which country had abolished it, but not long after that, as the economic situation changed, the estate tax returned. This is temporary, policy reduction and decline. However, this is not the case with the reduction of costs. Today, the burden of value-added tax will be reduced, and the economic situation will change in two years. We will restore the original pattern of value-added tax and restore the reduced tax to its original level again. This is obviously not possible. Therefore, the cost reduction must be sustained, must be through the reform of the tax system. According to this, if we conceptually divide it into inclusive and structural ones and define it as counter-cyclical adjustment and supply-side structural reform, the current tax cut and reduction in fees and charges are defined as counter-cyclical adjustment and supply-side structural reform. When applying this principled slogan and formulation to substantive operations, it is necessary to be careful, meticulous and professional, otherwise it is likely to be counterproductive and fail to achieve the desired objectives. At present, China's economic situation is in the short-term and long-term, internal and external, structural and cyclical contradictions, and these problems intertwined with each other, resulting in steady changes in economic performance, change in the excellent, which means that: The contradictions and problems we face today are at least two aspects: there are both short-term, external and cyclical contradictions and problems, as well as long-term, internal and structural contradictions and problems.

Therefore, the layout of China's macroeconomic policy cannot be unitary, and measures must be taken both in the face of downward pressure on the economy and in the face of the long-term task of supply-side structural reform. The supply-side reform should be carried out unswervingly. When reducing tax cuts to enable China's economic growth, we should give it two functions: on the one hand, it is countercyclical adjustment. On the other hand, it is endowed with the function of supply-side structural reform to ensure the realization of the goal of high-quality economic development.

B.2 By Professor Xu Xianchun

Director, China Economic and Social data Research Center, Tsinghua University

In 2018, China's economy remained stable, the growth rate of GDP slowed down, the consumer prices picked up, the producer prices retreated, and the growth rate of profits of enterprises dropped significantly, economic structure continued to improve, new dynamic energy continued to accumulate, and supply-side structural reform priorities continued to bear fruit.

First, from the point of view of production, China's economic operation shows the following characteristics in 2018

First, the value-added of the tertiary industry played a major role in stimulating economic growth; second, the growth rate of the value-added of the three industries has fallen down over the previous year; third, in the case of steady growth of GDP, the growth rate of added value in some industries fluctuated greatly.

(1) The added value of the tertiary industry played a major role in economic growth in 2018. GDP grew 6.6%, of which the added value of the primary industry increased by 3.5%. The added value of the second industry increased by 5.8%, and the added value of the tertiary industry increased by 7.6%. Obviously, the growth rate of the added value of the tertiary industry is the highest, and it played a major role in the growth of GDP. In 2013, the added value of the tertiary industry began to exceed the added value of the secondary industry, and in 2015 it exceeded half of the GDP. It accounted for 51.6, 51.9 and 52.2% of GDP in 2016,2017 and 2018, respectively. The added value of the tertiary industry has been increasing continuously, and it has been playing an important role in driving economic growth in recent years.

Which industries played a major role in the growth of the tertiary industry? The first sector was transport, warehousing and postal, with an increase of 8.1% in value added; the second sector was information transmission, software and information technology services, with an increase of 30.7% in value added; the third sector, rental and business services, with an increase of 8.9% in value added. The growth rate of each of the three industries was 7.6% higher than that of the tertiary industry. These three industries are closely related to the new economy and new dynamic energy. The rapid growth in transport, warehousing and postal services is influenced by the faster growth of the express delivery industry, which is closely related to the e-commerce. Information transmission, software, information technology services, leasing and business services are belonging to the new economy. It can be seen that the new economic momentum played an important role in the growth of the tertiary industry.

The new economy is growing fast. High-tech manufacturing, for example, grew 11.7% in value added. However, the share of new economic value added is still relatively small. New economic value added, released by the National Bureau of Statistics, accounted for 14.8, 15.3 and 15.7% in 2015, 2016 and

2017, respectively. As a result, while the new economy has maintained rapid growth, it has not reversed the impact of the traditional downturn on overall economic growth because of its small size.

(2) The growth rate of the added value of the three industries has fallen down in 2018. The growth rate of the added value of the primary industry dropped 0.5% points over the previous year, and the growth rate of the added value of the secondary industry dropped 0.1% points. The value-added growth rate of the tertiary industry fell 0.3% points. Because the added value of the tertiary industry is relatively large, the decline of the growth rate of the added value of the tertiary industry has a greater impact on the fall of the GDP growth rate. Among the tertiary industry, only the growth rate of information transmission, software and information technology services rose significantly, which was 30.7%, up 8.9% points over the previous year. The financial industry grew 4.4%, unchanged over the previous year. Other industries grew at a slower pace than the previous year. There are five industries down more than 1% point, the largest decline is the real estate industry, down 2.8% points.

(3) While GDP maintained steady growth, the growth rate of value added in some industries fluctuated considerably. GDP grew 6.8, 6.7, 6.5 and 6.4% in the four quarters of 2018, respectively. Economic growth slowed steadily on a quarter-by-quarter basis. However, the volatility of value-added growth in some industries was relatively obvious. The highest growth rate in the construction industry was 6.1% in the quarter, and the lowest growth rate was 2.5%, a difference of 3.6% points. The highest growth rate in the financial sector was 6.3% and the lowest growth rate was 3.1%, a difference of 3.2% points, while the highest growth rate in the real estate industry was 4.9% and the lowest growth rate was 2.0%, a difference of 2.9% points. The highest growth rate in information transmission, software and information technology services was 32.8% and the lowest growth rate was 29.1%, a difference of 3.7% points.

Second, from the demand point of view, economic operation shows the following characteristics in 2018

Consumer demand growth rate has picked up and its contribution rate to economic growth has increased significantly; investment demand growth rate has dropped, and its contribution rate to economic growth has declined. The growth rate of net export demand declined, and its contribution to economic turned to negative.

First, the growth rate of consumer expenditure has picked up in 2018. Per capita consumer spending rose 8.4% in nominal terms and 6.2% in real terms, up 1.3 and 0.8% respectively over the previous year, according to household surveys by the National Bureau of Statistics. Second, the growth rate of public service expenditure and the government consumption expenditure has both picked up. Consumer demand contributed as much as 76.2% to economic growth, up 18.6% points over the previous year. The contribution of consumer demand to economic growth rose significantly over the previous year, both because of a rebound in consumer demand growth, as well as a slowdown in investment demand growth and a shift in net exports from positive growth in the previous year to negative growth. The contribution rate of consumer demand to economic growth is relatively variable.

In terms of investment demand, first, the growth rate of total fixed capital formation was somewhat lower than that of the previous year. The nominal growth rate of fixed asset investment (excluding farmers) fell to 5.9% in 2018 from 7.2% in 2017, and the real growth rate also fell. At the end of 2018, inventories of industrial finished goods of large enterprises increased by 7.4%, down 1.1% points over the previous year, and the inventory growth rate has slowed down. The growth rate of total fixed capital formation and inventories has fallen down. Therefore, the growth rate of investment demand has slowed down. Investment demand contributed 32.4% to economic growth in 2018, down 1.4% points over the previous year.

Net export demand declined and its contribution to economic growth turned to negative. According to Customs Statistics, exports of goods rose 7.1% and imports rose 12.9%, and trade surplus fell 18.3%. Export demand contributed −8.6% to economic growth in 2018, down 17.2% points from 8.6% in the previous year.

In terms of demand, consumer demand contributed 76.2% to economic growth, while investment demand contributed 32.4% to economic growth. Taken together, domestic demand contributes 108.6% to economic growth. The consumer demand played a major role in stimulating economic growth.

Third, from the income point of view, economic operation shows the following characteristics in 2018

The per capita disposable income of the national residents has maintained steady growth, though its growth rate has dropped a little; the growth rate of total profits of large enterprises has dropped significantly. The national general public budget revenue growth rate has slowed down.

According to household surveys, per capita disposable income rose 8.7% in nominal terms and 6.5% in real terms in 2018, down 0.3 and 0.8% points respectively over the previous year. Total profit growth of industrial large enterprises reached 10.3% in 2018, down 10.7% points over the previous year. The main reason: first, the growth rate of main business revenue fell. Large enterprises of the main business revenue rose 8.5% in 2018, down 2.6% points over the previous year. Industrial producer prices rose 3.5% in 2018, 2.8% points lower than the previous year. Especially, when the increase in factory prices of industrial producers is large, the profit growth rate of enterprises tends to drop significantly. In 2018, the national general public budget revenue grew 6.2%, down 1.2% points over the previous year. Due to the slowdown in economic growth, price increases, corporate profit growth, and other factors, the growth rate of general public budget revenue fell back.

This paper summarizes the characteristics of current economic operation from three angles: production angle, demand angle and income angle. At present, the new economy, new energy development faster, such as high-tech industries, strategic emerging industries, some emerging industrial products, online retail has maintained a rapid growth. However, the size of the new economy is relatively small, has not yet reversed the impact of the traditional economic downturn on the overall economic growth. The industrial structure continues to improve, the proportion of tertiary industry is rising, the proportion of high-tech manufacturing industry is also rising, the demand structure continues to improve, the contribution rate of consumer demand to economic growth is further increased, and the investment of high-tech industry keeps increasing rapidly. The income distribution structure continued to improve, the actual national disposable income distribution continued to tilt towards residents, and the relative income gap between urban and rural residents continued to narrow. Overall, at present, China's economy as a whole maintains a stable state of operation.

B.3 By Professor Jia Kang

Chief Economist, Huaxia Institute of New Supply Economic Research

The theme of this meeting is to cut taxes, reduce fees. Enterprises, taxpayers, and members of the community are particularly concerned about how to lighten the burden. In addition to further lowering the positive tax, it is also necessary to reduce the fees. What kind of tax reduction and fee reduction mechanism must be considered in order to increase the vitality of economic and social development?

The research results of Xiamen University focus on and analyze such a major problem, and on the basis of emphasizing it as a theme in the discussion. There is a relative shortcoming in this report, which clearly points out that the social insurance contribution rate should be reduced properly in our country, but there is no further discussion on how to reduce the social insurance contribution rate. On this issue, I would like to talk about some of my own views.

First of all, it is necessary to reduce the social insurance contribution rate, and there is a clear consensus in this respect. Social insurance contributions, although there are some differences across regions, they add up to nearly 40%. In horizontal comparison with international economies, the ratio is clearly among the highest. Therefore, previous studies have repeatedly emphasized that such a level should be considered for downward adjustment, which is related to China's dynamic high-quality development on the road to modernization, which related to the enterprises as the main market.

Second, there is clearly room to lower social insurance contribution rate with a related question: how can China, as a developing economy, push the real burden of social insurance to the highest level in the world? We should admit the achievements in the construction of the social insurance system, and there are still obvious shortcomings. The discussion must be combined with the proposition of China's reform. China's reform has entered a deep-water zone, where problems crying to be resolved are all difficult ones, though we have discussed the problem of reducing the burden of social insurance for many years. Because of the vested interests, the resistance has been tenaciously demonstrated for more than a decade, and despite the fact that it is felt necessary to take measures to reduce social insurance contribution rate.

Thirdly, according to the direction put forward by Xiamen University report, I think that to reduce the social insurance contribution rate, we must innovate the mechanism under the direction of reform, and solve the problem of how to operate the key problems. Among them, the core content is to integrated the basic pension social insurance contribution funds to the whole society as a whole. This is a hard bone, but I think it must be chewed. There is now a chance to nibble down the hard bones. This is the supporting measure introduced by last year's individual tax reform, which clearly unifies the administrative responsibilities of all basic pension social insurance contributions to the tax authorities. The tax authorities found that there are about three forth of the basic pension social insurance contributions are not paid in place. Will the tax authorities recover their previous arrears? The problem caused a stir. It is necessary for the prime minister and authorities to make it clear that they are not allowed to go any further. Because the reasons for the outstanding payment of enterprises are too complex, it is certainly not feasible to recover the previous arrears.

However, in principle, no more burden can be added to the enterprise, and the fuzziness of expression follows. For example, where should I draw this line without burden? Are those above the medium level not to add to the burden, and those below the medium level still have to raise the burden? It is also impossible to reduce to the minimum. Therefore, the key is to make the system operational. Overall, this has given rise to a clear urgency to reduce social insurance contribution rate-despite the difficulties and problems that lie ahead. However, it is also a chance that we cannot ignore the operation of the mechanism which has not been properly rationalized for many years.

I would like to emphasize in particular the principle and significance of the overall mechanism. The overall plan of basic pension social insurance is to form a cistern, the payment entering the cistern together, produces the function of mutual aid. This kind of co-ordination has long existed, but after efforts in the past, it only reached the level of co-ordination at the provincial level. It has not been able to continue to advance for many years.

If the whole of China is a unified market, then, in principle, the most appropriate design should be to match the largest reservoir in the overall planning of the whole society, so that the function of mutual aid can be brought into full play, and many contradictions can be resolved. The prominent contradiction in the real society is that some provinces, such as the Northeast, spended more than their income. Support from the central government is necessary, in order to fill in the pension gap, so that old workers who should enjoy pension can get basic support in accordance with the standard. Another typical region is the Pearl River Delta. The age structure of the workers in Guangdong Province is quite young, and the water level in the cistern is rising higher and higher. After meeting the local payment needs, what about the extra part? we knew it was to entrust the money to the Central Social insurance Council, where they would invest on their behalf in order to increase their value. Ownership still belongs to Guangdong, and there is no possibility of allocating a penny of money to support the Northeast. This is the basic fact of the past: on the whole, there is already a pool mechanism for coordinating the basic pension fund, but because the cistern is fragmented, there is no connectivity. How can such a system overcome its shortcomings? Consideration should be given to logical expansion and to the promotion of overall social co-ordination.

However, will such an overall social co-ordination move the cheese from places such as Guangdong? Some people say that the income contributed by Guangdong Province has met the urgent needs of the northeast and will make the Cantonese suffer a loss. This is not true. In fact, Guangdong locals should not pay a cent of the basic pension fund, all should enjoy pension benefits in Guangdong. The standard is statutory, but these people collect water together in cisterns in accordance with the rules, and in the course of mutual aid, if the pool is large, the function will be enlarged to ensure that everyone is in accordance with the rules of law. Under the condition that the standard of payment and the level of income can be realized, the performance of the whole system can be improved, while the standard of payment and the burden of the enterprise can be reduced, which is the dividend brought by the reform. This reason is now a lot of people in the community do not understand. In order to increase the level of integration of this cistern and enlarge its function to support older workers who have contributed to the whole society in the past traditional institutions and transitional stages can receive pension benefits more smoothly, this overall co-ordination mechanism can be proved by both international experience and domestic practice, and will not lose the real interests of anyone in the overall planning system. Of course, there are differences in standards at present, after the standard is consistent in the future, can be calculated by sections, and the benefits can be clearly redeemed upon retirement.

To make this sense clear, decision-makers can make up their minds that after the management of basic pension fees has all been returned to the tax department, the whole society of the basic pension can be realized. In fact, after the collection of fees is under the control of the tax authorities, this matter has become a Pareto improvement in which some people benefit but no one is damaged in the reform of China, and after the improvement of the patrician function of the cistern, The standard of social insurance burden represented by the basic pension contribution can be lowered down in order to relieve the realistic dilemma faced by the three forth outstanding payment. Now, as long as the rate standard is reduced, a large number of enterprises will be freed, and the standard can be reduced, the payment of enterprises and individuals will be affordable.

We should acknowledge the contribution they have made in the past, and now they are working with everyone to improve the social insurance contribution that have been paid for about one forth pension social insurance contribution in the past. In my opinion, these are all very worthwhile to continue discussion, strive to form a basic consensus, take advantage of the trend to find the operational path and essentials, and urge the departments to make up their minds to include our suggestion in the Twelfth five-year Plan and the Thirteenth five-year Plan. But so far, the overall reform of the whole society for the basic pension has been put into practice.

B.4 By Professor Zhang Ping

Vice Director, Research fellow, National Finance and Development Laboratory

First of all, I would like to talk about my understanding of this report. I fully agree with the importance of lowering the social insurance contribution rate, especially in the scenario simulation, to reduce the social insurance contribution rate and use it to increase the income of the residents, so that a better and sustainable growth can be achieved and economic structure can be improved. High-quality growth contains two aspects: one is to improve the quality of life; second, innovation. By reducing the share of the government in the initial allocation, China can truly make people's lives better by transferring it to the residents; tax cuts will be transferred to companies, giving enterprises room to innovate and high-quality growth to be achieved. I recognize the logic of high-quality growth in China from this distribution perspective.

In terms of fee reduction and tax cuts, I think the first thing to do is to lower nominal taxes and rates. Now the collection has come up, first of all, to reduce the tax and fees of the name rate. Because the tax and the rate are set high, all the collection makes the enterprise overburdened. Second, I agree with the fiscal reform that Professor Jia Kang has been talking about. In 2019, the urbanization rate in China was 60%. In the past, there should be fundamental changes in the pattern of tax payment based on industrialization, and the share of tax revenue from the industrial sector in the tax revenue has been declining. While spending on social insurance and public services continues to grow, the 1994 tax reform, which now accounts for more than 80% of public-service spending, overlooks revenues. The original land finance to make up, how to compensate in the future, we must obtain further tax sources, especially to the taxpayer and its enjoyment of public services should be matched, which is the most important characteristics of the fiscal under urbanization. Third, the fairness of the tax burden, at present, all the tax burden on the enterprises, although individuals also bear the inside, but there are no provisions imposed on natural persons, natural persons do not know the obligations and powers of taxation, this is not equal. Moreover, the enterprises are overburdened, but the service enjoyed are insufficient. At present, the collection of VAT is carried out in the production link, and there is no asymmetry and inequities in paying taxes and enjoying services.

I think one of the biggest challenges in 2019 is a proper fall in PPI, a negative shift in the real economy, and a return to deflation. Judging from January's data, PPI growth was only 0.1%. From the current trend, it is possible for PPI to turn negative in June, and the negative characteristics of PPI are more obvious. M2 was discussed in the forecast, and the M2 growth rate rose to 8.4% in January, a good situation. But M1 grew only 0.4%, a big gap between M2 and M1, which has been a problem that China has been unable to achieve broad currency and tight credit. At present, the cash flow of enterprises is extremely difficult. M1 reflects the active state of the economy. If the economic activity does not rise and will not rise by the second quarter, then after the PPI turns negative, China will enter another round of deflation. This is an aspect worthy of our attention.

There has been a recent policy breakthrough in finance, which has been effective. Now the money is released, but the two-track system of the interest rate is a serious problem. Inter-bank interest rates have been falling, but loans have not fallen. Bank-to-bank loans are getting cheaper, while foreign loans only float up and down because of planned specified interest rate, which makes money rich, but does not drive foreign lending rates according to market rates.

Secondly, banks have a lot of money, while non-bank financial institutions are very short of funds due to the requirement of bank returns, which leads to a distortion in the allocation of China's dual finance. The recent policy of the central government has made some breakthroughs, that is, the way to issue bonds to banks to solve the problem of bank capital, so that for the first time an intermediary agency has a proper capital replenishment model. This model, in turn, matches the (TLAC) system of the G-20's total loss absorptive capacity, resulting in China's new policy of allowing intermediaries to replenish capital and absorb losses caused by economic fluctuations in the interest rate policy of lending. This policy is likely to strengthen China's financial stability at this stage.

Finally, the coordination of fiscal policies and financial policies. If China wants to cut taxes and reduce fees and build infrastructure, it will have a relatively large fiscal deficit. The urgent task is to actively issue municipal bonds, government bonds, and make transitional adjustments in the form of debt, so as to adjust the economy. The monetization of U. S. Treasuries is a path to fiscal and financial co-ordination, of course, which requires the transformation of China's fiscal system to overcome soft budget constraints in order to be healthier in coordination.

B.5 By Professor Chen Yanbin

Vice dean of the School of Economics, Renmin University of China

In response to today's topic selection, I would like to make some comments on the current fiscal policy. The 2018 government work report proposes the implementation of a positive fiscal policy. Whether the 2018 fiscal policy is sufficiently positive or not is an important subject for my discussion.

Support for fiscal policy has weakened in 2018, with the government budget accounting for four account books. The growth rate of general public budget expenditure in 2018 was relatively slow, with 6.8% growth in January-November. Compared with the same period in 2016 and the same period in 2017, the downward pressure on the economy in 2018 was increased by 3.4% points and 1% point respectively compared with the same period in 2016 and 2017. In particular, the external shock pressure caused by the China and the United States trade frictions was relatively large. But the general public budget expenditure growth rate of decline is more obvious. Further, from the point of view of the growth rate of various sub-items of fiscal expenditure, the growth rate of fiscal expenditure in areas closely related to people's livelihood, such as education, social insurance and employment, health care and family planning, has significantly slowed down. Compared with the same period in 2017, it fell 3.9, 8.6 and 3.7% points respectively. After adding up the general public budget expenditure and government fund expenditure (net of cost expenditure), we can conclude that the growth rate of the two types of fiscal expenditure since 2018 is lower than that of the same period in 2017. In January-November 2018, the growth rate of the two types of fiscal expenditure was lower than that of the same period in 2017. The combined increase in fiscal spending between the two categories was 8.5%, compared with 9.2% in the same period in 2017. Overall, as a result, fiscal spending in 2018 was significantly lower than in 2017.

Further examine the wide-caliber fiscal expenditure, that is, quasi-fiscal. The financing of government-backed agency bonds is expected to be roughly the same as in 2017, but the net financing of urban investment bonds and policy bank financial bonds has declined significantly. In January-November 2018, the combined amount of three "quasi-fiscal" expenditures was 1.31 trillion yuan. Compared with 1.87 trillion yuan in 2017, the decline was more than half that of 3.03 trillion yuan in 2016. This shows that quasi-fiscal supervision in 2018, has effectively reduced the risk of local debt, but the intensity of quasi-fiscal decline. PPP, the number of new projects and landing projects have dropped significantly quarter-by-quarter.

Further check the macro tax burden. Both narrow and wide caliber, the macro tax burden rose significantly in 2018, up from 2017 and 2016, and the value was at a six-year high. This shows that the burden reduction is insufficient is insufficient, and the effect is not very good. We can see that there has been some downward pressure on macro-economy in the past two years, but the function of counter-cyclical adjustment of fiscal policy is not enough. Tax cuts must come to fruition to prevent this part of the tax from being reduced, and the other part of the tax has come up again. This is the key to macro-policy to let the overall macro-tax burden fall, not just for certain sectors.

To prevent and resolve the local government debt risk, we should start with the mechanism and system, instead of using the tightening fiscal policy to reduce the local government debt. Fiscal policy should focus mainly on economic operations, counter-cyclical adjustment of economic volatility, promote short-term economic growth, and prevent the economy from falling too fast. At the same time, the local government debt reform is carried out from the mechanism system and the medium-and long-term perspective to prevent and resolve the local government debt. These are two different tasks based on different short-term and long-term perspectives respectively, and any fiscal policy cannot simultaneously defusing long-term debt and stabilizing short-term economic volatility

B.6 By Professor Yang Zhiyong

Vice Director of Degree Committee, Institute of Financial and Strategic Studies, Chinese Academy of Social Sciences

I mainly talk about the understanding of tax cut and fee reduction. First, both macroeconomic policy choices and reforms are supportive of comprehensive, inclusive tax cuts and fee cuts. As to what to do to reduce controversy, we can draw some inspiration from past reforms and policy implementation. For example, there is some controversy at first, but we can optimize some concrete measures. The personal income tax policy, which began in October 2018, is possible for some low-and middle-income earners, such as taxi drivers in Beijing who earn 8000–10,000 a month. But for a particular group, it doesn't matter to him how to cut taxes and fees.

All government measures come at a price. We cannot expect the Government to provide more and better public services and collect no money. Under this premise, on the one hand, we should guarantee the expansion effect of the policy, on the other hand, we should also guarantee the normal operation of the government. If spending is austerity, then the expansion effect will certainly be affected.

Government expenditure from three aspects, there is almost no room for personnel funds, and may not be a lot of debt. A lot of public funds are not enough. There may be some room for current account funding. Everyone acquires that the current account budget of this year is a little more than that of the last year. There are many difficulties.

What if we have to cut taxes and cut fees, and things have to be done? There needs to be a safeguard mechanism. Where can we find the safeguard mechanism? We are now using common bonds. When it comes to local debt, there is a focal point in it. If we want to expand local debt, which is the central government to the local limit. The question is, how should the quota be given? In the past, the financial situation in the western region was relatively tight and should be given a little more. The debt is to be repaid, some places say, the central government has given the target, I borrowed money did not want to pay back. At the same time, we carry out the policy of expansion, in return for a poor mechanism.

Our country is very special, some places have very tight financial resources, they need to do a lot of things. For example, Northeast China, just mentioned the issue of social insurance pension, if what Mr. Jia Kang said can be realized, it is very perfect, we look forward to this. Go to Hainan Island in winter to see if the Northeast people really have no money, money has been transferred, can you say no impact? This year the Guangdong Province announced the budget report is more detailed, the social insurance expenditure growth is very large. In terms of overall goals, the national labor market is unified, but there is a lot to be done about how the transition is going to take place. For example, how can the contribution made by the elderly in Northeast China be reflected? in the past, his low wages formed the assets of local enterprises in the northeast, and those assets were more directly related to their contributions. Can we consider allowing state-owned assets to be converted into a way to form cash flow? The solution to this problem will be more secure.

There is still room for improvement in reducing taxes and fees. I've been talking about reducing taxes and fees for years, but how much has it been? Last year, it was 1.1 trillion, and then it was 1.3 trillion. Since it is an active fiscal policy to cut taxes and fees, whether there can be a package of tax cuts, how much will be cut this year and how much next year, there is a very useful expectation, and a lot of controversy can also be avoided. The transparency of tax cuts is further enhanced, telling the common people what we have done, how much VAT has been reduced, how much has it been reduced, how many tax rates have been reduced, how many articles have been listed. how much individual income tax cuts, how much corporate income tax cuts, give a simple package, this may be better than the annual calculation of the effect.

The real estate tax has been discussing. If this is a tax increase measure, then in the context of overall tax cuts and lower fees, the issue of the timing should also be considered. At the same time consider its impact on national governance, such as many uncertainties in the market. In the long run, real estate tax should push house prices up more. If it brings uncertainty to the market, a lot of measures in the process of pushing, less tax resources will not achieve the desired effect, whether it can be properly considered later.

When it comes to macroeconomic regulation and control, it is inevitable to mention fiscal operation. Will there be better factors in 2019? We have seen some positive factors in the course of China and the United States economic and trade negotiations. If domestic economic reforms can boost economic growth in 2019, it can boost income growth in the context of tax cuts.

For local governments, tax revenue is more to ensure the operation of the industry. Local governments rely heavily on land transfer income, and life will be easier if many of the land problems can be solved. But land and real estate are closely related. In the past, real estate prices continued to rise with monetary factors, land supply factors, and expectations for house prices. If the ratio of income to house prices is not reasonable, and one day no one will follow, then the general trend of falling house prices will be unstoppable.

B.7 Professor Lou Feng

Research Director, Institute of quantitative Economics and Technology Economics, Chinese Academy of Social Sciences

Our judgment on economic growth is as follows: in the first quarter of 2019, China's GDP growth rate will decline to about 6.3%, the second and third quarters will be a full-year low, and the fourth quarter will pick up slightly. This year's economic growth in general showed a decline.

Logically, there are the following reasons: first, from the supply side, China's potential GDP growth rate has been declining continuously in recent years, which is closely related to the reduction of China's labor force population and the decline in total factor productivity (TFP), and so on. It is inevitable that the economic growth rate will continue to decline in 2019, which is in line with the development trend of its potential economic growth rate.

Secondly, from the perspective of aggregate demand, on the one hand, there are many favorable factors for investment in 2019, such as the introduction of a more active investment policy in infrastructure, with a more active fiscal policy and sound monetary policy. There are still some weak links in China's infrastructure investment, fixed assets investment still has a large space for development. We note that China's approval of high-speed railway, airports and subways is accelerating in 2019, and real estate investment will continue to grow at a rapid pace. In terms of investment, the growth rate of fixed asset investment in new technology industry and modern service industry is very high. Although the investment growth rate of industry is slowly declining, the overall quality of investment industry is rising, which means that China's economic growth has a solid foundation for growth.

On the other hand, there are also some disadvantages to the investment. For example, the investment of state-owned enterprises is not high. Since June 2018, the growth rate of investment of state-owned enterprises has been negative, about −3.2% for the whole year. In addition, there are some worries about investment in manufacturing industry. At present, manufacturing industry mainly faces three problems: overcapacity, declining profit margin, and negative impact of China and the United States trade friction. Compared with 2017, 11 of the 18 industrial sectors continued to increase in 2018, accounting for more than 60% of the total, indicating that the problem of overcapacity in China is still increasing. Total profit margins for industrial companies grew 10.3% in 2018, nearly halving from 21% in 2017, which will constrain the increase in manufacturing investment growth in 2019. In addition, the negative impact of China and the United States trade friction on investment comes mainly from aggregate demand. In the past decade or so, one of the important factors in China's rapid economic growth has been the rapid growth of exports, which has led to rapid increases in employment, production capacity and investment, as a large amount of exports will produce a great deal of demand. We have done policy simulations using dynamic GTAP, and the results show that if the current trend evolves, trade frictions between China and the United States will reduce manufacturing investment by 1.4% points and employment by 8 million people. Therefore, the trade frictions between China and the United States will have a significant negative impact on investment, which is expected to grow by about 0.3% this year.

In terms of consumption, the growth rate of consumption in the past decade or even has been a mild decline. Favorable factors include the escalation of consumption, the introduction of individual tax reform last year, new consumption sustained expansion and so on. The negative factors include the rising ratio of household debt, which will slow down the driving force of future consumption, and the education, health care, health care and other industries in China is far from enough to meet the needs of the society. Consumption growth rate in 2019 is expected to decrease 0.3% points over the previous year.

In terms of import and export, although China's openness to the outside world is increasing, international cooperation is gradually deepening, and the trade structure is also constantly transforming (the growth rate of product exports in high-tech industries is significantly higher than that in ordinary industries), and so on. However, the biggest uncertainty of China's foreign trade in 2019 is the trade friction between China and the United States, which has become the main negative factor affecting China's exports. According to our policy simulation, China and the United States trade frictions will bring China's exports to about 5.7%, down 4.2% points over the previous year.

In terms of policy recommendations, we propose that strengthening innovation is fundamental to promoting reform and opening-up. With the slowdown in economic growth, China's economy is developing in a high-quality direction, which depends on innovation and technology, not simply on extensive development models such as investment. We should promote ownership reform, further reduce macro-tax, improve manufacturing innovation ecosystem, enhance manufacturing innovation ability, and drive the innovation transformation of manufacturing industry.

MIX
Papier aus verantwortungsvollen Quellen
Paper from responsible sources
FSC® C105338

If you have any concerns about our products,
you can contact us on
ProductSafety@springernature.com

In case Publisher is established outside the EU,
the EU authorized representative is:
Springer Nature Customer Service Center GmbH
Europaplatz 3, 69115 Heidelberg, Germany

Printed by Libri Plureos GmbH
in Hamburg, Germany